World Scientific Lecture Notes
in Marketing – Vol. 1

Customer Xperience Leadership

A Blueprint to Maximize Performance

World Scientific Lecture Notes in Marketing

Series Editor: Chezy Ofir *(The Hebrew University of Jerusalem, Israel)*

**World Scientific Lecture Notes
in Marketing – Vol. 1**

Series Editor
Chezy Ofir
The Hebrew University of Jerusalem, Israel

Customer Xperience Leadership

A Blueprint to Maximize Performance

Nadav Goldschmidt
The Center of Xperience Leadership, Israel

W⟡ World Scientific

NEW JERSEY · LONDON · SINGAPORE · BEIJING · SHANGHAI · HONG KONG · TAIPEI · CHENNAI · TOKYO

Published by

World Scientific Publishing Co. Pte. Ltd.

5 Toh Tuck Link, Singapore 596224

USA office: 27 Warren Street, Suite 401-402, Hackensack, NJ 07601

UK office: 57 Shelton Street, Covent Garden, London WC2H 9HE

Library of Congress Cataloging-in-Publication Data
Names: Goldschmidt, Nadav, author.
Title: Customer xperience leadership : a blueprint to maximize performance /
    Nadav Goldschmidt, The Center of Xperience Leadership, Israel.
Description: Hackensack, NJ : World Scientific Publishing Co. Pte. Ltd., [2024] |
    Series: World Scientific lecture notes in marketing ; volume 1 |
    Includes bibliographical references and index.
Identifiers: LCCN 2023007513 (print) | LCCN 2023007514 (ebook) |
    ISBN 9789811264085 (hardcover) | ISBN 9789811279492 (paperback) |
    ISBN 9789811264092 (ebook for institutions) |
    ISBN 9789811264108 (ebook for individuals)
Subjects: LCSH: Customer relations. | Marketing. | Leadership.
Classification: LCC HF5415.5 .G657 2023 (print) | LCC HF5415.5 (ebook) |
    DDC 658.8/12--dc23/eng/20230418
LC record available at https://lccn.loc.gov/2023007513
LC ebook record available at https://lccn.loc.gov/2023007514

British Library Cataloguing-in-Publication Data
A catalogue record for this book is available from the British Library.

For any available supplementary material, please visit
https://www.worldscientific.com/worldscibooks/10.1142/13077#t=suppl

Desk Editor: Geysilla Jean Ortiz

Typeset by Stallion Press
Email: enquiries@stallionpress.com

Foreword

There is no doubt that the success of any company, small or large, is positively correlated with the level of customer experience being delivered. Outstanding experiences lead to tremendous success while poor experiences lead to curtailed suboptimal success.

This positive correlation was true thirty years ago and it's going to be true thirty years from now. Executives and managers know it and invest resources toward improving the experiences that their companies deliver. Yet, the results are often disappointing. Companies have a difficult time consistently fulfilling customers' expectations and satisfying their needs over time. Especially in the digital era we live in, where things move faster than ever and customers expect businesses to be accessible anywhere, anytime.

From my over thirty years of experience as President and Chief Executive Officer of academic medical centers, I can honestly say that the major hurdle in delivering exceptional care experiences is the lack of knowledge and know-how in this area. This isn't exclusively for healthcare-related hospitals, but for every industry that's caring for the public. Companies lose tens of billions of dollars every year because of it.

Most executives and managers went through academic studies in a variety of universities majoring in finance, strategy, marketing, operations, etc. They learned the ins and outs of those topics which allowed them to execute on a high level. Customer experience wasn't part of the curriculum. They might have taken a course or two on this topic, but they didn't specialize in it. As a result, key service-oriented skills and abilities are missing from executives' and managers' toolbox. This hinders their ability to build customer-focused organizational systems and service-centered processes and procedures that are crucial to creating positive experiences.

Nadav got his Ph.D. from Cornell University, specializing in Service Management. During his degree, he studied this topic from top to bottom, linking it to organizational behavior and human resource perspectives. His research focuses on the DNA of companies that provide the optimal experiences in the world. For the past twenty years, he has been teaching a variety of customer experience courses in a variety of higher education institutions. He also works with companies to improve their relationships with customers and use service management tools to maximize success. Nadav's vast knowledge of customer experiences is clearly conveyed in this fascinating book.

The interdisciplinary book in front of you offers a clear blueprint for anyone looking to improve customer experiences. It includes fourteen lectures. Every lecture outlines one component of the blueprint and together offers a path to customer experience leadership. The components are explained in a simple, organized, vivid, straight-to-the point manner. Practical tools and easy-to-implement customer-focused actions are outlined. Readers can go through the book cover to cover or just read and learn about a specific component they want to improve.

Read the book, execute what is written, and propel your team, department, or organization to the top of the customer experience leaderboard. To enhance performance, boost customers' and employees' satisfaction and engagement, thereby vastly improving financial results.

Improving customer experiences isn't an easy journey. Considerable time, effort, and work must be invested. But it's worth it. The return on investment is substantially higher than the other alternatives out there. Don't try to execute the entire book at once. Go lecture by lecture and take the time to do it right. Improving experiences is a journey and a commitment from the top of the organization; it is essential for success.

Kevin M. Spiegel, FACHE
Chief Executive Officer, Crozer Health
Assistant Professor, Drexel University College of Medicine

Contents

Introduction

The 4D Xperience Model

> "*A customer is the most important visitor on our premises, he is not depend-ent on us. We are dependent on him. He is not an interruption in our work. He is the purpose of it. He is not an outsider in our business. He is part of it. We are not doing him a favor by serving him. He is doing us a favor by giving us an opportunity to do so.*"
>
> **Mahatma Gandhi**

The digital, mobile, and social media world we live in has dramati-cally changed the business landscape in many ways. Probably the major change is the shift in power from companies to customers. In the past, customers were completely dependent on the company's goodwill before, during, and after the purchase. The company decided what information customers received, the place of the transaction, and the time it happens (i.e. opening hours).

Today, this is no longer the case. Customers are gaining control and don't need the company's help to make educated decisions. They can go online and find all the information on the company, its products, features, quality, prices, and what the competition are offering. They decide where the transaction will take place (home, road, work) and when (any time, 24/7/365).

Customers have options to choose from (domestic companies, nationwide, and around the globe). If one company doesn't respond or adjust to what customers ask for, switching to another company can be done almost instantly. This is especially true for the younger generations who are nothing like their parents. They are tech-savvy, connected, better informed, aware of choices, and aren't afraid to make a change and try new things.

An Interesting Fact

It's estimated that companies lose between $130,000,000,000 (130 Billion dollars) to $1,600,000,000,000 (1.6 Trillion dollars) every year in the U.S. because of poor customer experience [1, 2].

Another change of the hyper-connected, fast-paced world is the commoditization of products and services. Once every few years a new, groundbreaking product (iPhone) or service (Streaming) comes along to the market and creates a great buzz. But this is the exception, not the norm. Usually, it's more about enhancing or modifying what is currently available. Even with a new offering, the company could bank on less than a year before competitors catch up and customers can't tell the difference. In such a business environment, companies have a difficult time differentiating themselves from the crowded marketplace and becoming commoditized. This is where customer experience comes into play.

Research shows that customer experience is more important than products and prices, in today's battleground for a competitive advantage and long-term success [3, 4].

- In total, 70% of customers choose a company to interact with and be loyal to based on the experience received.
- A customer is four times more likely to leave a company if the problem is experience-related rather than price or product-related.
- Almost half (47%) of customers say they will stop buying from a company if they have a subpar experience.

- It's noteworthy that, 91% of customers who are unhappy with a brand will leave without complaining.
- Finally, 76% of customers say it's easier than ever to take their business elsewhere.

All in all, customers want experiences. They look for them and have options. If they are unhappy with one option, they leave. Often, without saying anything. That is a major issue for companies. Staying competitive is getting harder and harder.

Customer experience isn't a new concept. In 1998, *Harvard Business Review* published an article titled "Welcome to the Experience Economy." The article forwarded the idea that experiences are the new frontier for growth to the economy and competitive differentiation for companies. Since then, many companies ignored this message and continued doing business as usual. Great service is elusive and the number of companies delighting their customer is small [3].

There is a simple way to demonstrate this point. When people are asked to recall a great experience that they had, it often takes them some time to think of such an event, if they can even remember one. Adversely, asked to recall a bad experience, and often several stories instantly come to mind.

In yesterday's world, ignoring customer experience and still succeeding might have worked. Now, disruptor companies in every industry are lurking for these vulnerable old-school companies providing mediocre experience. Companies continuing on the same path, doing more of the same and doing it even more efficiently, will see lower returns on investment and poorer business results. They eventually become irrelevant and risk survival. Delivering experiences is no longer nice to have, but a must have for long-term success.

Amazon, Lululemon Atletica, Sephora, Emirates, Trader's Joe, Singapore Airlines, IKEA, Warby Parker, Publix Supermarkets, REI Coop, Starbucks and even an airport — Changi Airport — are examples of industry experience leaders that top customer satisfaction surveys and are considered great places to work. They create engaged employees who are service-oriented and motivated to serve customers.

These companies come from different industries and have different business models. However, all these companies have one common theme — they beat their competition and show amazing financial results. Their success stems from obsessive focus on experiences. Yes, these companies sell products and services, high quality products and services. But the way they lead the industry and beat the competition is by the hospitality given to customers. It's through the helpfulness, friendliness, personalization, and convenience that customers crave. Customer experience is the show, the main event. The services and products are the stage and props.

These businesses live and breathe both sides of the experience. They are laser-focused on providing amazing value for customers — creating a great customer experience (CX) and are fixated on constructing a great place to work for employees — creating a great employee experience (EX).

These companies understand that CX and EX are equally important. They are two sides of the same coin and are intertwined. Both are needed to ensure the company's long-term success. One without the other creates imbalances that hurt the company performance and results.

Consequently, a simple, yet powerful equation emerges:

$$\text{CX (Customer Xperience)} \times \text{EX (Employee Xperience)} = \text{CS (Company's Success)}$$

Focusing on CX without attending to EX will lead to labor issues, inefficiencies, and poor experience to customers. The opposite isn't much better: Focusing on EX without attending to CX will end up providing customer the wrong things, at the wrong place, at the wrong time.

The companies mentioned above also never stop learning, always innovate to improve the offering, and distance themselves from competitors. Customers love these companies. They become loyal, willing to pay higher prices, and evangelize them to friends, family, and even strangers online. This combination is a powerful engine of sustainable, profitable growth that leads to financial results that far exceed competitors that aren't customer-obsessed.

An Interesting Fact

Customer-centric companies are 60% more profitable than companies that aren't [1].

The importance of customer experience to success has made it a leading topic of discussion in executive suits. Companies invest substantial resources to improve experiences. But the results are disappointing. This usually happens when there is lack of understanding and sponsorship of the specific concept (in this case, customer experience). Consequently, companies want to move forward with experiences, it's that almost half don't know how [5].

To make great customer experience a reality, people have to understand the different components required to make it happen. The different components are illustrated in a model called the 4D Xperience Model depicted on the next page. The model serves as the blueprint for this book.

Part one of the model helps the reader understand customers and what they want. Parts two and three help understand how to design and deliver experiences that customers want. Part four helps understand how to constantly improve the experience and keep customers happy. Here is a quick peek of each part.

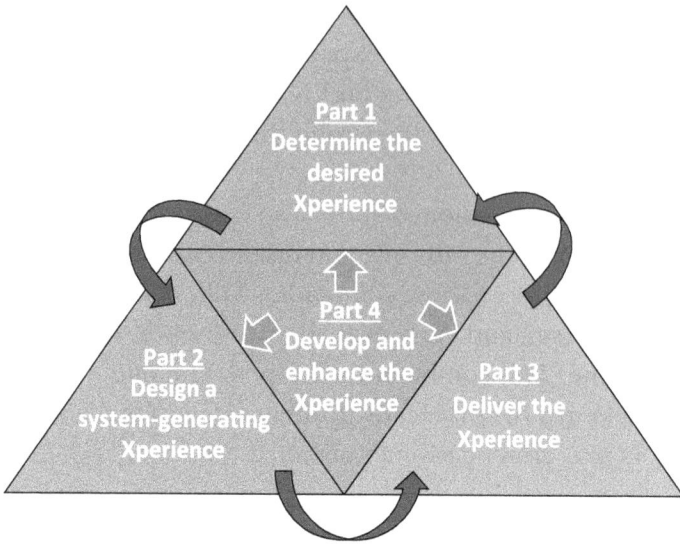

The 4D Xperience Model
Determine - Design - Deliver - Develop

Part 1 — Determine the desired Xperience

Customers set a certain level of expectation from any company they plan on contacting. Then, they interact with the company and evaluate the encounter. That evaluation is then compared to the initial expectations and the level of satisfaction is determined. Learning the three components — expectations, interaction, and perceptions — serves as the basis on which every company should design its organizational system.

Part 2 — Design a system-generating Xperience

The organizational system has to translate customer expectations into system-wide, cross-functional operational actions. Every aspect of the organizational system must focus on creating value for customers and making their journey as simple and easy as possible.

Part 3 — Deliver the Xperience

Whether the experience is delivered through technology or by humans, it has to be friendly, seamless, effortless, and consistent across all touchpoints, channels and devices. It should be an experience that fulfills and even exceeds customer's expectations.

Part 4 — Develop and enhance the Xperience

Customer experience has to constantly evolve and improve. There are ample ways to develop and enhance it: Do things better, come up with new ways, or fix intrinsic problems. Sticking to existing ways and resisting change in a rapidly changing world is a losing formula.

This book outlines in detail each of the four parts. It aims to enable executives, managers, consultants, students, and anyone who deals with customers in any area or discipline to become a customer experience leader.

References

[1] Planview Blog (2017). 8 Customer Experience Stats Every Leader Needs to Know. Available at https://blog.planview.com/8-customer-experience-stats/

[2] Call centre Helper (2018). Not Valuing Customers Costs Us Businesses $136 Billion Every Year. Available at https://www.callcentrehelper.com/not-valuing-customers-costs-136-billion-132902.htm

[3] McGinnis D. (2019). 40 Customer Service Statistics to Move Your Business Forward. Available at https://www.salesforce.com/blog/customer-service-stats/

[4] Clark D. (2012). Why is Great Service so Rare? Available at: https://www.forbes.com/sites/dorieclark/2012/08/01/why-is-great-service-so-rare/?sh=2321a566649a

[5] Staffaroni, S. (2019). The Top 4 Customer Experience Challenges and How to Overcome Them. Available at https://www.getfeedback.com/resources/cx/the-top-4-customer-experience-challenges-and-how-to-overcome-them/

Part 1

Determine the Desired Xperience

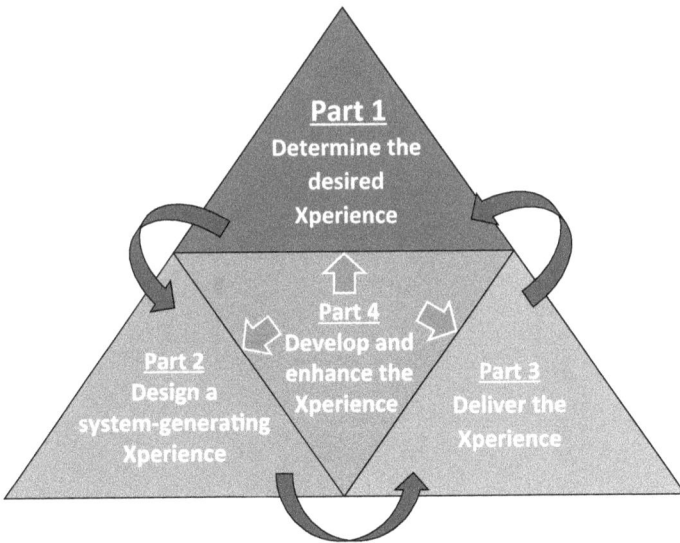

The 4D Xperience Model

Albert Einstein once said "If I had an hour to solve a problem and my life depended on it, I would use the first 55 minutes determining the proper questions to ask."

The success of any institution around the globe (public, private, non-profit or even a single-person business) depends on understanding customers' frame of mind and the experience created during the service encounter. That understanding starts by asking three fundamental questions:

1. What is customer experience?
2. Why invest in customer experience?
3. What do customers want?

Discussing and answering these questions provide paramount information needed to figure out and interpret the customer experience concept. They help discover the different dimensions and learn in-depth about the most important person everyone is working for — the customer. Lectures one, two, and three provide answers to the three questions presented above.

Lecture 1

What is Customer Xperience?

"We see our customers as invited guests to a party, and we are the hosts. It's our job every day to make every important aspect of the customer experience a little bit better."

Jeff Bezos

The terms "customer experience" and "customer satisfaction" are often used interchangeably. Although both terms express an outcome, they are meaningfully different.

Customer satisfaction is a specific outcome of an encounter with a company. It's one piece of the puzzle. It shows the level of enjoyment that customers have from a specific encounter with a company. For example, satisfaction with the company's website, billing statement, or face-to-face interaction.

Customer experience is a more holistic concept of the whole company. It's the entire puzzle. It shows the overall perception and feelings the customer has towards the company and a full assessment of the quality of its brand. It's a perception that stems from all interactions with as well as exposure to the company. The perception is based on many elements and encounters that occur over time. Every interaction leaves a good or bad impression and thus has a positive or negative impact. When most of the interactions are positive, a superior experience is created which, in turn, leads to a fan-like feeling and loyalty to the company.

The way a customer feels about the company determines his or her current and future behaviors and actions. A positive feeling goes beyond satisfaction. It results in making customers come back, repurchase, and advocate the company by referring it to their friends and family, creating a loyalty bond towards the company. A negative experience leaves customers dissatisfied. Consecutive negative experiences lead to a combination of negative emotions — anger, upset, annoyance or frustrations. Such feelings can lead customers to retaliate against the company by taking their business elsewhere or shaming the company by posting damaging reviews.

Customers make daily decisions about what products and services to buy and from whom to buy. Some decide according to a specific brand name while others base their decision on price. For most customers, the experience they expect to receive determine their decision. They choose convenience and honesty, speed and courtesy, professionalism, and reachability over price and even the brand's name.

A Good Example — Apple Store

The company's stores, which are also referred to as "The Experience Store", sell beautiful products. But the main focus is on delivering emotional experience, like the Genius Bar.

Every interaction is personal, intimate, and customer-specific. The goal is to delight customers, build long-term rapport, and get positive word-of-mouth instead of making short-term transactions. Each customer gets the same experience whether they purchase or not.

This is the reason why over one million customers visit Apple's stores globally every day.[1]

Customers have an abundance of choices. They choose high value over low value more often. The value can be emotional (the way they are treated) or rational (they get what they wanted).

Customers determine value by taking the total benefits received from the transaction (tangible and intangible) and divide it by the total cost paid (price, time, effort, uncertainty and inconvenience). When the company or its people take actions that are important, useful or worthwhile for customers, the value grows. A high value leads to great experiences.

Value can be created in many ways. In the following pages, ten value creation pillars are outlined. No pillar is more important than another. The more pillars a company delivers upon, the more exceptional the experience.

Pillar 1 — Transparency

The customer has to trust the company before he or she does business with or become loyal to the company over time. Transparency is a great tool in building a customer's trust. Without transparency, customers are skeptical about every move the company makes and if it has their best interest at heart, making interactions frustrating.

Transparency is about telling customers the truth: Straightforward, without misleading information, asterisks, or fine print. It's about providing customers with all the information needed to make the right decision and get the best possible solution. For example, providing customers with a comparison of the company's products and services with competitor offerings. Companies can try to conceal information or confuse customers. But customers do their research before contacting the company and they eventually find the incriminating material. Providing the necessary information upfront creates trust. It shows that the company believes in what it sells and the value it creates.

Transparency keeps customers in the know — What is done, how long it will take, and when it will happen. Customers appreciate not being kept in the dark and knowing a problem happened or a mistake occurred. When customers are informed about these issues and what is done to fix the situation, they respect the company and trust it. Excuses, half-truths, lengthy explanations about what can't be done or just ignoring the customer in these situations are examples of anti-transparency actions.

A Good Example — Patagonia
This outerwear company provides transparency throughout its supply chain. The company wants to show its customers that it avoids any environmentally-unfriendly practices by showing videos on its website displaying the way its products are produced.

The customer can click on each video and see each step in the production process, including all textile mills and sewing factories used to create each item. The company invites feedback from customers on ways to improve the processes.

Pillar 2 — Professionalism

Customers expect companies to provide the best possible solution to their request or problem, doing everything mistake-free the first time while explaining what is done and why. They don't want to run around trying to find the "right" person who has the expertise to help. Customers are willing to wait a little longer if it means they get someone that takes care of everything efficiently, from start to finish.

Customers do research before interacting with the company. They are knowledgeable. Having less than expert service providers is a receipt for poor experience. Intelligent service providers can provide customers with crisp explanations about the company's offerings and take care of any issue that arises. Customers feel they are in good hands and perceive the company as highly professional, reducing uncertainty and increasing calmness.

Pillar 3 — Convenience

We live in an era of convenience. Customers can do more and more through their smartphones even when at home. They can consult with a doctor and have their checkups done online. They can download forms sent by a company, digitally fill and sign them, and send them back. They can order lunch or coffee, decide which branch and what time to pick it up, no waiting required. They can order any product and have it sent to their homes. Convenience.

Convenience is about making the service interaction as easy, effortless, and comfortable as possible for the customer (see Figure 1.2). It starts with letting customers interact with the company anywhere (at home, at work or on the road), anytime, on any device (smartphone, smartwatch, tablet, etc.), across different service channels (Email, Chat, Facebook, etc.). This makes it easy for customers to find what they need and make the purchase as smooth as possible. This ends with helping customers get the product or service quickly up and running while fixing any post-purchase issues flawlessly.

The company doesn't know the customer limitations or specific situation. By allowing customers to do it their way, on their own terms, the company maximizes convenience and limits the waste of

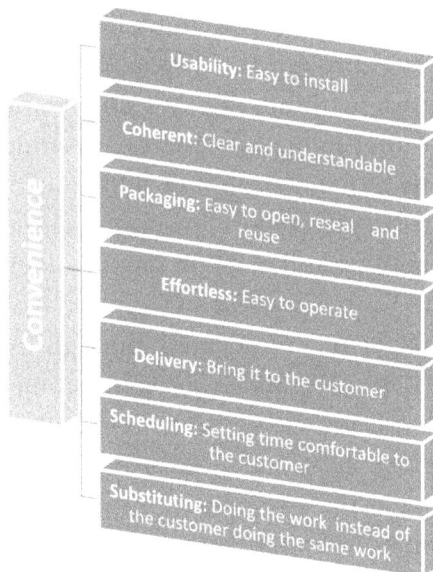

Figure 1.2. Example of Convenience

time and energy. Customers appreciate and value it. In contrast, when the company raises the customer's inconvenience, causing them to put forth more effort in every interaction, alternatives become attractive and churn quickly follow.

Pillar 4 — Simplicity

Simplicity is about making everything easy for the customer to understand or do. It's about getting the basics right. Taking away the intricacy and complexity that is usually associated when dealing with legal systems, bureaucracy, and unfriendly processes. Customers shouldn't have to overthink, struggle, be confused, redo, reread, or ask clarifying questions. When information is presented in short, simple terms, and without jargon, it's easily understood. When forms are uncomplicated, signs are readable, and only intuitive actions are required, things are simple and doable. An easy to navigate website that allows the customer to find what they need with a few clicks, without help, is the embodiment of simplicity.

What is simple for one customer might be complicated to another. Thus, the company has to think like the average customer and build everything through their eyes. If the common customer doesn't understand something, then it's simply not simple enough. For example, car rental companies are usually straightforward when it comes to picking up and dropping off the car. However, other aspects such as the dizzying array of insurance and refueling options are much more complex and difficult for customers to understand. Similarly, in Health Care companies, customers have a difficult time understanding aspects such as selecting the right coverage and payment of claims. Complex issues leave customers helpless and stressed which often leads to poor outcomes and dissatisfaction.

Organizations that continue to favor outdated rules and procedures while not fixing flaws in operations will be facing significant difficulties. Watching, listening, and looking at customers interacting with the company at every touchpoint is an effective way to simplify the experience.

Pillar 5 — Speed

Everything is getting faster. Faster cars. Faster internet. Faster communication. Technological developments have opened many opportunities to improve speed in dealing with customers. Service providers can work faster, communicate immediately with customers, find the necessary information quickly, and have data analyzed on the spot. This allows the company to provide real-time responses and faster resolutions.

Amazon, Uber, and others have fundamentally changed the mindset when it comes to doing things quickly. They have shown the ability to speed up interactions without sacrificing the level of quality. Amazon has moved from a three-day delivery to next day and same day delivery. Uber has made ordering a ride done quickly, on the spot, with limited to no waiting time.

A Good Example — Mayo Clinic

Patients fly in from all over the world for the healthcare provider's time-compressed care that can usually provide a definitive diagnosis and sometimes initial treatment, including major surgery, within three to five days. Mayo refuses to settle for the sluggish, unreliable timeline common in other hospitals. The process is built in a way that most scans are read on the spot, allowing doctors to verify the scan while they are still at the patient's side and decide if another scan is necessary. Customers receive a quick diagnosis and the clinic provides a great experience and improves its operations.[2]

Pillar 6 — Personalization

Each customer is different with distinctive needs, wants, schedule, and limitations. The era of "one-size-fits-all" is concluded. The era of "one-size-fits-one-customer" has started. By following each customer history of interactions with the company, data is collected on customer behavior, actions, likes, dislikes, and more. This information enables personalizing interactions to the tone, style and actions that best fit each customer's individuality. Over time, more information is gathered which enables the company to anticipate requests and thus fit future interactions more accurately. That is called "mass customization" and it's powerful.

Customers don't just want personalization — they often demand it. The advancement of technology has led customers to expect more from companies. They dislike getting irrelevant information or offering. They have enough information "noise" around them. Customers know companies are collecting their personal data. Most don't mind as long as it's kept private and used to know what they need and provide relevant suggestions and valid recommendations. Customers feel frustrated when website content isn't personalized or if the person who answers the call doesn't know their name. Companies that are able to personalize the interaction get the customer's attention. It's estimated that up to 35% of Amazon purchases come from personalized recommendations the company makes to its loyal customers [3].

An Interesting Fact

According to the consulting company Accenture, 75% of customers are more likely to purchase from a company that knows their name and recommends them products and services based on their purchase history [4].

Clothing brand Stitch Fix personalizes the clothes and accessories it sends each customer while Netflix does the same for movies. Several airlines are providing tablets to customers with their pre-ordered individualized shows and movies. Hyundai provides personalized information on its website. When a customer wants to compare crossover SUV models, he or she gets a landing page that showcases the company's cars compared to other brands on key features. Another customer interested in the inventory of a specific Hyundai model is directed to the website of the dealership nearby to check for its availability.

When personalization is done well, customers feel the company really knows them best and provides the best possible option. Suddenly the interaction is great, and the experience is wonderful. This usually inspires intense positive emotions and passion toward the company.

Pillar 7 — Friendliness

In an era of rising technology where customer care is delivered more and more via automated systems, friendliness still plays a deciding factor in how customers perceive the company's value. The scarcer human interaction becomes, the more valuable it gets. More than 70% of customers say that friendly service providers is one of the factors that makes them "fall in love" with a brand [5].

A great customer experience or a bad one usually doesn't revolve around the product or service bought. Rather, it's simply a reflection on how friendly the interaction with the company's personnel was. Friendliness is about being kind, caring, helpful and supportive. Providing customers a genuine human touch shows respect and creates an emotional connection. It makes them feel special, important, appreciated, and not just a number or a "dollar sign". It lets them know someone is there, willing to help — no ifs, ands, or buts.

Pillar 8 — Reachability

Customers don't wake up in the morning thinking "Which company should I call today?" They contact the company only when they need assistance. At that moment-of-truth when the customer really needs help, if the company is easily reachable — without barriers and friction on the customers' preferred channel — value is created. Lifelong loyalty can be achieved. Companies that are prepared for these moments find ways to be reachable.

With the variety of channels that exist today — social media, chat, email, and self-service — it should be easy to reach a company. Thus, when a company is unreachable at the moment-of-truth, nothing else matters. Telling customers to "call later", "we currently can't respond to your inquiry", "waiting time is longer than usual", or "we are closed, comeback tomorrow", are value annihilators. With no response, all the good that the company did for the customer in the past is quickly forgotten.

An Interesting Fact

Customers who use multiple channels (omnichannel) are more valuable than customers who use a single channel in several aspects. These customers spent 4% more on every shopping occasion in the store and 10% more online. With every additional channel used, the shoppers spent more money in the store.

In addition to bigger shopping baskets, omnichannel shoppers were more loyal. Within 6 months after an omnichannel shopping experience, these customers had logged 23% more repeat shopping trips to the store and were more likely to recommend the company [6].

Pillar 9 — Extra Mile

Customers expect companies to effectively deal with any question, problem, or issue raised. Doing the expected is fine and customers will probably be satisfied. But it won't make anyone excited. To create value, companies have to go the extra mile and positively surprise customers. Do more than expected by going beyond the common response or solution. Give customers something they didn't ask for or didn't know was an option. It isn't about grand gestures, but doing the small things and taking simple actions that make a big difference and causes customers to say WOW. Going beyond expectations can't happen in every situation. It's about seizing the right opportunities to do something special for customers.

To go the extra mile, companies have to get their people to take initiatives and be proactive. Making the first move sends a powerful message to customers that the company has their best interests at heart. Customers perceive such actions as thoughtful and appreciate the time and effort it saves them.

Pillar 10 — Consistency

Consistency is about achieving a level of performance which doesn't vary greatly in quality over time. Customer value consistency because it reduces uncertainty and unpleasant surprises. When customers know the company always keeps its promises and delivers the same high-quality performance no matter the situation, they perceive it as a reliable choice which increases their confidence and trust.

Customers understand and accept that no business is perfect and there are occasional missteps and variance in actions that lead to inconsistency. They don't accept random performance that at one time is excellent and another time is poor. Big swings in the level of performance leads to greater variability in the experience which leaves a negative impression and causes concern among customers about future interactions.

Consistency has to be across people, departments, and channels. That is tricky. People can provide a consistent level of experience when they have a similar level of knowledge, skills, and abilities. Departments can deliver consistent levels when they break down silos across the company and make policies and rules clear for everyone to follow. The company can achieve consistency across channels when it embraces every channel, invest in it, and makes sure the same level of experience is provided through each one. Finally, consistency is about doing the same things over time and not in intervals.

Consistency is about paying attention to details and making sure every aspect of the customer's journey is up to the organizational standard. When everyone plays by the company's rules and sticks to its standards, consistency is achieved, and value is created.

An Interesting Fact

Research shows that 9 out of 10 customers expect to receive a consistent level of customer service [7].

Conclusion

In the internet, mobile, and social world, switching companies is easier than ever. All it takes is just a click of a mouse. Customers can do a quick search and instantly get several options to buy with price comparison, inventory availability, and delivery dates. With such a variety of choices, customers look for companies that offer more, do more, and provide more. They focus on the experience provided rather than the price asked for.

Customers look for companies that focus on them and make their lives easier. They want companies that listen, understand what they need, and guide them toward picking the best possible option. By doing this, companies present themselves as a trustworthy, reliable option that customers can count on.

Providing high value is the key ingredient in getting customers to buy, come back, and reduce churn. Every company provides high value at one time or another. The best companies constantly provide high value by understanding and delivering the elements discussed in this lecture.

References

[1] Farfan, B. (2019). Apple's Retail Stores Around the World. Available at https://www.thebalancesmb.com/apple-retail-stores-global-locations-2892925#:~:text=These%20are%20impressive%20numbers%20considering,Parks%20around%20the%20world%20combined

[2] Mayo Clinic (2022). Mayo Clinic Proceedings Vol 6 (2). Available at https://mcpiqojournal.org/article/S2542-4548(18)30046-8/fulltext

[3] Mackenzie, I., Meyer, C., and Noble, S. (2013). How Retailers Can Keep Up with Consumers. Available at https://www.mckinsey.com/industries/retail/our-insights/how-retailers-can-keep-up-with-consumers

[4] Tsernov, K. at Qminder (2020). The Future of CX: 14 Customer Experience Trends for 2020 (and Beyond). Available at https://www.qminder.com/customer-experience-trends-2020/

[5] Wiita, A. (2019). Never Underestimate the Importance of Friendly Customer Service. Available at https://workingsolutions.com/never-underestimate-the-importance-of-friendly-customer-service/

[6] Sopadjieva, E., Dholakia, U.M., and Benjamin, B. (2017). A study of 46,000 Shoppers Shows that Omnichannel Retailing Works. Harvard Business Review. Available at https://hbr.org/2017/01/a-study-of-46000-shoppers-shows-that-omnichannel-retailing-works#:~:text=The%20more%20channels%20customers%20use%2C%20the%20more%20valuable%20they%20are&text=After%20controlling%20for%20shopping%20experience,online%20than%20single%2Dchannel%20customers

[7] Live & Learn Consultancy LTD (2021). What is Customer Service? Available at https://www.liveandlearnconsultancy.co.uk/what-is-customer-service/

Lecture 2

Why Invest in Customer Xperience?

"There is only one boss. The customer. And he can fire everybody in the company from the chairman on down, simply by spending his money somewhere else."

Sam Walton

The level of customer experience can make or break a company. No matter how good or affordable the products or services it sells, if the customer doesn't enjoy the encounters with the company, they won't stick around. Customers have more and more options and they can afford to be picky.

On the road to making a profit, companies place short-term sales over long-term relationships and loyalty. The reason is simple. Sales quickly bring in revenue. These initial purchases lead to short-term profits and success. However, through building long-term relationships and loyalty, the company ensures cash flow, constantly improves revenues, and thus doesn't just make a profit but maximizes it (see Figure 2.1 on the next page).

This short-term, long-term battle that executives have is a major barrier to delivering experiences. Short-term focus brings the CEO into direct conflicts with the interest of customers. Long-term results are sacrificed for short-term outcomes. It's rarely possible to consistently create and deliver delightful experiences while trying to

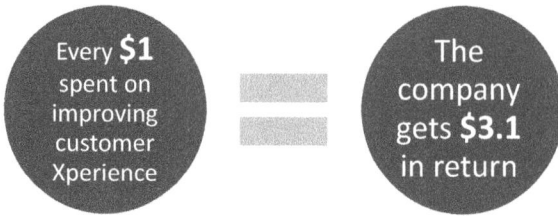

Figure 2.1. The ROI on Customer Experience Improvement [2]

maximize quarterly profits because delighting customers may reduce short-term profits. Faced with choice, most executives are incentivized to focus on short-term. Most executives admit to sacrificing the future of the company in order to meet short-term shareholder values and stock market whims [1].

One way to show how customer experience influences long-term profits is through stock performance. As shown in the box below of An Interesting Fact, a portfolio of customer experience leading companies in the US have achieved cumulative returns much higher than the S&P 500 — the five hundred biggest companies in the US.

An Interesting Fact

A portfolio of customer experience leading companies showed a cumulative return over 10 years of 312%.

The S&P 500, the five hundred biggest companies in the US, achieved 205% at the same time.

A portfolio of customer experience lagging companies have achieved a cumulative return of just 98% during the same period [3].

Another study from 2000 to 2014, showed that the cumulative gross returns on customer experience focused companies amounted to 518% while the S&P 500 grew by 31% over the same period [4].

Purchases and profits are the applause that customers give companies they enjoy doing business with. Delivering superior experiences is the best strategy to not just get applause, but a "standing ovation". Superior experiences get the most "applause" because they are able to influence both sides of the profit equation concurrently — increase revenue and decrease cost. McKinsey found that on average, companies that improve customer experience increase revenues by 10–15% and lower cost by 15–20% [5].

Let's take a closer look to see why this is the case.

The Customer Xperience–Loyalty–Revenue Growth Connection

Revenue growth is the increase of company's sales between periods. It provides an indication of the health of the company's ability to sell things to customers. A Bain & Company analysis shows that companies that excel in customer experience, grow revenues 4 to 8 percent above their market [6].

Forrester found that customer experience leaders achieve higher compound average revenue growth of 17 percent over five years, way over the 3 percent achieved by those providing poor experience [7].

The correlation between customer experience and revenue growth stems from customer loyalty (Figure 2.2). Experience leads to positive loyalty which leads to revenue growth [8] .

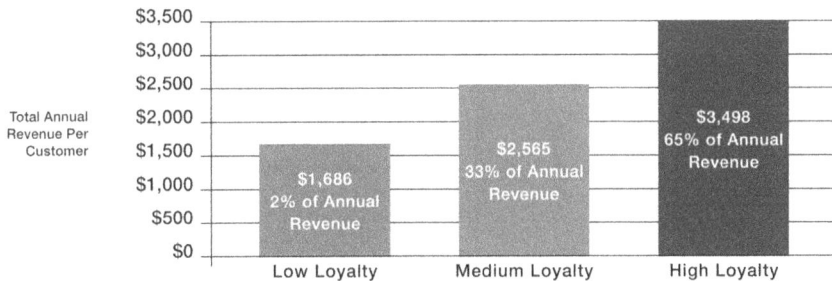

Figure 2.2. Customer Loyalty and Revenue Per Customer

Source: https://customerthink.com/a-new-way-to-measure-customer-experience-and-its-financial-impact

Specifically, positive loyalty leads to the following positive outcomes:

Increase purchases — Loyal customers increase purchases over time. Loyal customers are five times more likely to repurchase, five times more likely to forgive a mistake or other failures and continue to purchase, four times more likely to refer other people, and seven times more likely to try a new offering [9]. A different study found that the top 10% of loyal customers spend three times more per order than the bottom 10%, and the top 1% of customers spend five times more [10].

There is a direct correlation between the amount of time a customer has been shopping with a company and the amount spent per visit. In Figure 2.3 for example, apparel shoppers purchased 67% more per order after shopping with a company for 30 months than they spent on their initial purchase [11].

Attracting new customers — Loyal customers spread positive word-of-mouth (WOM) and positive online rating [12]. Each time a

Figure 2.3. Amount Spent by Customer Over Time

Source: Bain & Company/Mainspring Online Retailing Survey (No. 2116), December 1999

customer makes a purchase they become more comfortable with the company, and thus are more willing to make a positive referral (Figure 2.4). Bain found that after 10 purchases, repeat shoppers refer 50% more people to a store than a one-time purchaser. By attracting new customers, repeat customers actually increase the company's profitability [13].

Figure 2.4. Number of Purchases Impact on Customers' Reference

Source: Bain & Company/Mainspring Online Retailing Survey (No. 2116), December 1999

Positive WOM and high rating eliminates the first thread of doubt that most prospective customers have, thus increasing conversion rate among customers. The higher the conversion, the higher the revenue.

Receiving premium prices — customers want to pay as little as possible when they see no value in the offering. Loyal customers are loyal because they get high value. They are willing to pay for that value (see Figure 2.5 on the next page). A survey indicated that 68% of customers would pay more to the company that provides great service. Another 33% would pay 1–9% more, 27% would pay 10–20% more, and 8% would be willing to pay over 20% more [14].

Another study done by PWC based on 15,000 global respondents found that customers would pay up to 16% more for a company that delivers a superior experience [15].

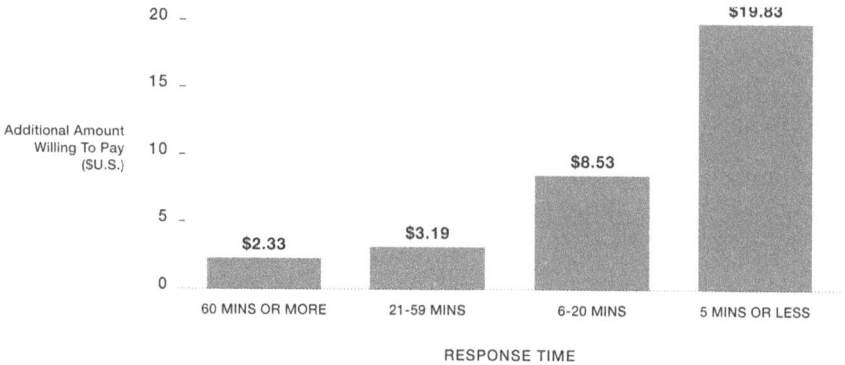

Figure 2.5. Response Time to Customer Complaints and Willingness to Pay

Source: Wayne Huang *et al.*, "How customer service can turn angry customers into loyal ones", HBR, January, 2018

The Customer Xperience–Loyalty–Reduce Costs Connection

Any company can reduce its costs. But there is a positive reduction and a negative reduction. A positive reduction is about making things more efficient and effective, reducing expenses without negatively influencing customers, employees, managers and the system. A negative reduction is the opposite — reducing expenses to maintain profits, disregarding everything and everyone.

Loyal customers lead to the following positive cost reductions.

Lower marketing and sales expenses — when loyal customers spread positive WOM, the company needs to spend less to attract new customers. Less marketing and sales efforts reduce costs. Attracting new customers today is becoming harder and harder given the fierce competition online. Companies increase sales and marketing spending just to get the same result they did in the past. Loyal customers limit this additional cost.

Reducing customer churn — given that it costs five to ten times more to get a new customer than it is to keep a customer, a lot of money is saved when customers are loyal. It's also cheaper to serve loyal customers because the company already knows them and how to treat them effectively.

Minimum failures and repeat service — A superior customer experience eliminates many unpleasant surprises, disputes and misunderstanding between the company and its customers. This, in turn, limits the number of failures and mistakes along the way. The cost of dealing with mistakes that anger customers and require compensation and repeat of the service is slashed. In other words, a superior experience eliminates the cost associated with repairing mediocre service and rebuilding a relationship with dissatisfied customers.

Lower legal, regulatory, and public relations costs — loyal customers forgive the company more often, avoiding the disasters of customers going to the media and making their negative story viral. It also helps avoid circumventing regulations or cutting corners, reducing the tremendous cost of legal issues and public relations crisis associated with poor experiences.

Increasing digital usage — loyal customers are more inclined to accept the company's advice and offer of receiving electronic billing and using self-service options more often. Digital usage reduces the company's cost-per-customer. A superior digital experience keeps customers using self-service channels, thus keeping cost low over time.

Lower service providers turnover — employees who serve loyal customers know them and build relationships with them. They are able to perform their job to the best of their ability which makes them happy and motivated. This reduces the level of churn among them and thus reduces turnover cost that stems from hiring and training new employees to replace those who left.

To sum up, customer experiences reduce costs in the following ways:

Lower marketing and sales expenses.
Reducing customer churn.
Minimum failures and repeat service.
Lower legal, regulatory, and public relations costs.
Increasing digital usage.
Lower service providers' turnover.

Conclusion

The law of demand states that pricing drives demand. High prices reduce demand while low prices increase it. In today's market, experiences drive demand much more than price. As shown in this lecture, there is a positive correlation between great customer experience, profitability, and the company's long-term success.

Great experiences yield benefits on both sides of the profit and loss statement. One side leads to engaged customers who are loyal, buy more, and refer others, leading to revenue growth. The other side reduces the cost of negative consequences, operating cost, and many service-related charges. All of which lead to lower costs. Companies that aren't able to deliver great experiences cap their financial results.

References

[1] Martin, R.L. (2011). Fixing the game. Boston, Harvard Business School Publishing, p. 99.
[2] Lumoa. (2021). Business Value and ROI of Customer Experience: The Step-by-step Guide. Available at: https://www.lumoa.me/blog/business-value-and-roi-of-customer-experience/
[3] Aksoy *et al.* (2008). The long-Term Stock Market Valuation of Customer Satisfaction. Journal of Marketing Vol. 72(July), 105–122.

[4] Fornell, C. *et al.* (2016). Stock returns on Customer Satisfaction Do Beat the Market: Gauging the Effect of a Marketing Intangible. Journal of Marketing Vol. 80 (September 2016), 92–107.

[5] Valdez, E. (2018). 5 Ways Customer Experience Can Influence Sales Growth. Available at https://www.chiefoutsiders.com/blog/customer-experience-sales-growth

[6] Debruyne, F. and Dullweber, A. (2015). The Five Disciplines of Customer Experience Leaders. Available at https://www.bain.com/insights/the-five-disciplines-of-customer-experience-leaders/#:~:text=Bain%20%26%20Company%20analysis%20shows%20that,make%20recommendations%20to%20their%20friends

[7] Manning, H. and Czarnecki, D. (2016). Customer Experience Drives Revenue Growth. Forrester, June 21. http://vkconsulting.gr/wp-content/uploads/Forrester-Customer-Experience-Drives-Revenue-Growth-21-June-2016.pdf

[8] *Ibid.*

[9] Glia (2017). Ways to Exceed Customer Expectations. Available at https://blog.glia.com/5-ways-exceed-customer-expectations/

[10] Big Commerce (2018). Ecommerce Metrics and KPIs You Should Measure (And Why They're Important). Available at https://www.bigcommerce.com/blog/ecommerce-metrics/#how-to-measure-ecommerce-success

[11] Baveja, S.S., Zook, C., Hancock, R.S., and Chu, J. (2000). The Value of Online Customer Loyalty and How to Capture it. Available at http://www2.bain.com/Images/Value_online_customer_loyalty_you_capture.pdf

[12] Burkard, K. (2016). Maximizing the Impact of Your Brand Advocates. Available at https://blog.smile.io/maximizing-the-impact-of-brand-advocates

[13] McEachern, A. (2020). What is a Repeat Customer and Why are they Profitable? Available at https://blog.smile.io/repeat-customers-profitable/

[14] Hyken, S. (2018). What Customers Want and Expect. Available at https://www.forbes.com/sites/shephyken/2018/08/05/what-customers-want-and-expect/#7ebaae427701

[15] Puthiyamadam, T. and Reyes, J. (2018). Experience is Everything: Here's How to Get it Right. Available at https://www.pwc.com/us/en/advisory-services/publications/consumer-intelligence-series/pwc-consumer-intelligence-series-customer-experience.pdf

Lecture 3

What Do Customers Want?

"*You have got to start with the customer and work backwards to the company.*"

Steve Jobs

More than 90% of customers say they would stop purchasing from a company after three or fewer poor service experiences [1]. This mind-boggling number is the reason why the number one question every company should ask is "What do customers want?".

Understanding what customers want isn't an easy task. Customers don't always know what they want; nor do they articulate it when they do know, much less share it with companies. Understanding what customers want can be done by "walking in their shoes." This entails observing how they interact with the company, listening to them, seeing what they go through, and trying to understand how they feel throughout the encounter. Advances in technology and analytics are making it possible to know what customers want without even asking them. The technology observes, follows, and listens to every step, action and decision they make. This allows the company to extrapolate what the customers need even if they themselves are unaware of it. This eliminates the gap between the experience customers actually want and the experience the company delivers.

Asking customers what they want and operating correspondingly is considered as an outside-in perspective. This perspective is about being customer-oriented, looking at the business from the customer's perspective (Outside), and subsequently designing the organizational system and offering accordingly (In). The company makes decisions based on what's best for the customer and offer value that meets and exceeds their needs.

Embracing the outside-in perspective allows the company to align itself with customers and thrive. It can set clear standards to operate and respond to customers' evolving preferences and even serve customers' unmet needs.

Many companies still have an inward focus bias known as inside-out perspective. This perspective focuses on the company's internal strengths and capabilities to effectively conduct operations, manage resources, and sell products (Inside) and less on the customer's specific needs (Out). The company is very effective but risks becoming irrelevant and losing opportunities to competitors that swoop in, offering great experiences.

Understanding what customers want requires an examination of three components:

- The experience journey
- Customer expectations
- Customer perceptions

In the following pages, each component is explained in detail.

The Experience Journey

Every customer who comes in contact with a company goes through a "Journey". The journey is the sum of steps that customers have to go through, digitally or physically, to get what they need. It starts with an initial thought about the company, goes through the process of engagement, and ends at the moment the customer leaves. The journey usually changes from one company to another and can include many touchpoints or only a few. At the end, the customer evaluates the journey they just went through.

To understand the customer's journey and consequently their experience, it should be mapped. The journey map diagram offers a visualization of the chronological footsteps that customers take to get the request or issue resolved. It shows how customers navigate across touchpoints and what obstacles and barriers they may encounter.

Each customer journey should be observed as a whole from start to finish. Look to see if it offers a seamless, efficient, frictionless journey. Unfortunately, companies often focus on individual touchpoint devoted to billing, service calls, website visit, product usage and the like. They fail to manage the multi-touchpoint, multichannel, end-to-end experiences that have the customer's overall view.

By continuously following the customer journey, companies can spot "points of strength" that make customers happy, and "points of pain" that include obstacles that lead to dissatisfaction (see Figure 3.1). These points become opportunities to enhance the experience and improve the journey. Specifically, companies can use the journey map to:

- Diagnose where failures occur or bottlenecks happen.
- Identify inefficient, ineffective, or unhelpful processes.

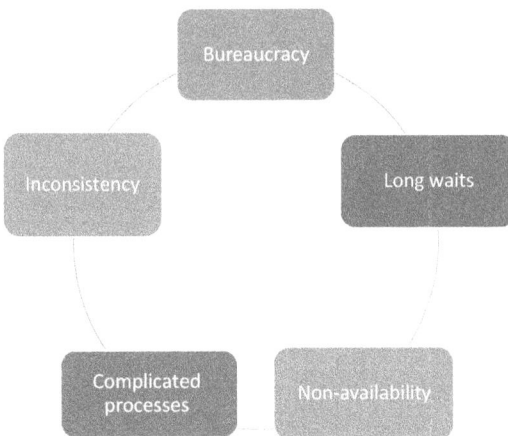

Figure 3.1. Points of Pain For Customers

- Better understand the usage of service channels.
- Show where customers are struggling, confused, or spending extra effort to get what they need.
- Uncover customer's changing needs.
- Understand customers' needs at different stages of the encounter.
- Highlight gaps between what customers expect to get and what they actually receive.
- Illustrate the flow of actions, emotions, and information from touchpoint to touchpoint.
- Create better best practices.
- Improve communications between departments and people.

A Good Example — Customer Journey

A customer sees an advertisement for a car loan (touchpoint # 1).

His father recommended (touchpoint # 2) the company in the advertisement because he had a good experience with them.

The customer goes to the company's website (touchpoint # 3) and uses the company's online car loan calculator (touchpoint # 4) to see if the repayments are affordable. Once the customer is convinced that the company is the right fit, they go to a face-to-face meeting in the branch (touchpoint # 5) with a service representative (touchpoint # 6). They fill the necessary forms (touchpoint # 7) needed to get the car loan.

After a couple of days, the customer receives an email (touchpoint # 8) with approval to the car loan. The customer opens the email and reads the contract with details, terms and conditions for the loan (touchpoint # 9).

The customer checks his bank account and sees that the money was received (touchpoint # 10).

The customer receives monthly payment statements (touchpoint # 11).

This journey example totals 11 touchpoints. There could be more touchpoints going back and forth during the engagement toward completing the transaction and after the conclusion of the transaction.

The journey described above might be considered by some customers as seamless and straightforward. But it's possible that other customers might feel that coming to the branch was unnecessary and everything could have been done online. Other customers might also be disappointed because the process of approving the application took too long (two days) and the discount the car dealer offered expired.

Remember, customers judge the experience they receive on every single touchpoint they come in contact with and the journey as a whole. A bad experience at a certain point might cloud the whole experience. Thus, every point must be designed to deliver a superior experience. Furthermore, a customer can be satisfied with several touchpoints and still be disappointed with the overall experience. That happens when the company does well on the touchpoint level but poorly on the journey level. Take new customer onboarding or existing customer contract renewal. How long is the journey? Does it require several back-and-forth phone calls and numerous web and mail interactions? If it does, then the touchpoints are fine, but the onboarding or renewal processes cumulative experience across the journey is poor.

The journey isn't static. It changes with the customer tenure and experience with other companies. As the relationship with customers develops, the map has to be adjusted and done periodically to see any changes that occur during the long-term relationship. This allows the company to optimize the customer's end-to-end journey and create the desired experience across all touchpoints, improving efficiency and reducing the cost of service.

This is where journey mapping is essential. By gathering feedback at each of the eleven touchpoints and the journey between the points, it's possible to understand the key moments that influence customer behavior and how each one contributes to their overall perception. The information can help companies improve the moments that matter most for customers and create a better, smoother, seamless journey. Perfecting journeys pays off in profit outcomes.

An interesting Fact

Companies that excel in delivering seamless journey tend to win in the market. Effortless and convenient journey correlates strongly with faster revenue growth, positive word of mouth, and loyalty [2].

"Maximizing satisfaction with customer journeys has the potential not only to increase customer satisfaction by 20% but also lift revenue up by 15% while lowering the cost of serving customers by as much as 20%" [3].

Consequently, the customer journey map should be like a poster, pinned to the office wall, and grabs people's attention. It tells the customer story in a simple, easy to understand way. It reminds everyone that the customer's needs must always be at the forefront of their thinking and actions. By glancing at the map, people should be able to see the key touchpoints that the customer passes through. This helps them understand how they influence customers and determine their experience.

The digital era is dramatically changing the journey composition. Today's multichannel, digital devices, and hypercompetitive markets make the journey more intertwined. The traditional face-to-face and phone journeys are becoming less favorable for customers. Today, journeys that are web-based and include Bots and other digital assistance devices like Alexa and Siri are the more popular option, especially for young people. In fact, 67% of millennials and Gen Z use voice-activated personal assistants to connect with companies. That is 70% more than traditionalists and baby boomers who do the same [4]. The reason is simple: The experience is faster, easier, and more satisfying.

In any Journey, customers determine the quality of the experience by comparing their expectations from the encounter (what they want) with their perceptions of the encounter (what they got).

A simple equation is formed:

- When perceptions = expectations, the customer is satisfied
- When perceptions > expectations, the customer is delighted
- When perceptions < expectations, the customer is dissatisfied

Let's take a closer look at customer expectations and customer perceptions to interpret how customers really think.

Customer Expectations

Customer expectations are predictions made by customers about the positive and negative events that are likely to come to fruition during the encounter. Expectations come first because they serve as a reference point against which the company's actual performance is evaluated. When the company meets customer's expectations and especially when it exceeds them, the experience is superior, and customers praise the company and provide positive word-of-mouth. When the company delivers something less than expected, customers are dissatisfied and frustrated which usually triggers negative word-of-mouth.

Every time a customer thinks about a company for the first time or the fiftieth time, they automatically have certain expectations from the interaction with the company. Expectations are formed in the mind of the customer, and thus, are subjective and unique to each individual. Two customers with similar profiles coming to receive the same service or buy the same product, may have totally different expectations depending on their history, preferences, and obviously their personality.

Expectations tend to be different across industries. Customer expectations from an insurance provider differ greatly from expectations from a hospital or hotel. Expectations also tend to be dynamic and can quickly change across different situations. There are a range of situational factors that may occur from the moment the customer decides they need the service until actually receiving it. Situational factors can be the weather, long waiting line, number of alternatives, a customer cutting inline, parking place, or time constraints.

In the past, customer expectations from companies were basic — have the product in stock, offer fair prices, and fix any problem that happens along the way. The internet, mobile, and social revolution created disruptive companies that set expectations on a much higher level especially with regard to time, professionalism, and transparency. Today, customers expect every company to offer convenience by serving them anytime, anyplace, and immediately.

An Interesting Fact

A good 90% of customers expect a response to their support questions within 10 minutes or less [5].

Expectations involve a paradox. When expectations are high, customers will come, but the chances of disappointments rise given the lofty expectations that have to be fulfilled. Low expectations, on the other hand, turn away customers from coming because they feel the company is inept; if they come, there is a high chance for a positive surprise and exceeding their expectations (this is known as under promise and over deliver).

Knowing what the customer expects allows the company to provide an offering that accurately fulfills those expectations and create a great experience. Without that knowledge, the company acts blindly, offering customers things and treating them in ways that might or might not work. This leads to poor encounters, wasted resources, and customer churn.

Finding out what customers expect is challenging and requires an investment of time and resources. But this is a worthwhile investment. It yields the most basic information needed to deliver superior experience.

Consequently, companies must make sure expectations are at an ideal level, a level that customers are happy with and the company is able to consistently deliver while maintaining a competitive advantage. To achieve this level, expectations have to be managed.

Managing expectations

Companies have to work with customers to set and steer their expectations to an optimal level for both sides — not too high and yet not too low. A level that makes both sides happy. Managing expectations happens at three stages:

- Before the encounter begins.
- While the encounter takes place.
- After the encounter ends.

Before the encounter begins — At this stage, customer expectations are set at the desired level. The pre-encounter set level of expectations act as a reference point on which everything during the interaction is judged upon. The level of expectations can be set by using the following tools:

- **Communication** — Outbound correspondence from the company (marketing, advertisement, social media testimonials, community involvement, etc.) notifies the customer of what to expect from the company.
- **Company's website** — Most customers' first encounter with the company happens on its website. The clarity, simplicity, and convenience of the website sets their level of expectations.
- **Online reviews** — Customers go online and search for information about the company they want to do business with. Testimonies and ratings they see — positive or negative — sets their expectations.

While the company can influence and manage customer expectations, it doesn't have complete control. There are factors outside the company's scope that impact and set customer pre-encounter expectations. One example is customer experience with other companies. People buy from many companies. If one company provides a great experience, expectations for other companies rise. Amazon's experience characterized by speed, friendliness, seamlessness, and personalization, set a higher bar for every other company. Companies that don't adjust to Amazon's standards will disappoint their customers and create dissatisfaction and attrition. Ironically, customers were happy with the level of service received from these companies before interacting with Amazon or other experience leaders.

An Interesting Fact

When asked, more than 60% of customers used the phrase "I want an Amazon-like experience." [6].

While the encounter takes place — At this stage, customer expectations are managed in real time and in a variety of service channels by steering them toward a level that can be met. That is done by the two entities that deliver the experience: Service providers and technology.

- **Service providers** — Listen to customers and understand their level of expectations at that moment. If the level is too high, they have to steer customers toward what can be done or provided rather than on what can't be done. Empathy, kindness, and personalization are effective tools to help do that.
- **Technology** — Steers customer expectations by telling them the steps they need to take to get what they need, guiding them throughout the process. Ensuring customers don't forget any step along the way and offering them options they didn't know existed.

After the encounter ends — At this stage, future customer expectations are managed. By staying in touch with customers, the company can build long-term relationships, fix mistakes, and thus determine the forthcoming level of expectations. This is done in several ways:

- **Follow-ups** — Using customer feedback surveys to understand which customer expectations weren't met. Then, working with those customers to fix what went wrong, steering their expectations toward an acceptable level.
- **Support** — When customers contact the company after the encounter with problems they face or additional questions they need to ask, support can steer their expectations. A quick and immediate response with a professional solution makes sure expectations stay positive.
- **Being proactive** — Initiating contact with customers and offering them something they want before they actually asked for it or even know they need it, is an effective way to steer expectations toward the desired level.

Far too many negative experiences boil down to unmet expectations. The customer expected one thing and the company delivered something else. This leads us to the second component that determines customer satisfaction and that is customer perception.

Customer Perception

Customer perception refers to customer awareness, impression, and opinion of a company as a whole and specifically its experience offerings. From the customer's point of view, the most vivid impression of the quality of a service occurs during the service encounter, also known as the "moment of truth." During the interaction, customers evaluate what they receive, how they are treated, and the service environment in which the interaction occurs. This evaluation, influenced by their senses and feelings, determines the quality of the experience received. Each additional encounter helps customers reassess and refine their positive or negative perception of the company and expectations for future service interactions.

Customers, not the company, determine if the experience was of high or low quality. It doesn't matter how much resources were put into providing the experience or what people within the company say about the quality. If the customer doesn't perceive it as high quality, it isn't.

The intangibility of service makes it tough for customers to evaluate its quality. Research done by Parasuraman, Zeithaml and Berry developed a measuring instrument called SERVQUAL [7]. The instrument has been widely applied in a variety of contexts and cultural settings and found to be relatively robust. It has become the dominant measurement scale in the area of service quality. Interestingly, the research done in the mid-80s has gone through some modifications over the years, especially with the rise of the digital era over the last decade. However, its core concept is still applicable today. SERVQUAL shows that customers perceive the quality of service received on five major dimensions:

- **Reliability** — The ability to perform the promised service dependably and accurately.
- **Assurance** — The knowledge and courtesy of employees and their ability to convey trust and confidence.
- **Responsiveness** — The willingness to help customers and to provide prompt service.
- **Empathy** — The provision of caring, individualized attention to customer.
- **Tangibles** — The appearance of physical facilities, equipment, personnel, and communication material.

The most important dimension is reliability. It makes sense. Customers first and foremost want the company to do what it said it will do. The other dimensions in the order of importance are: responsiveness, assurance, empathy, and tangibles. All dimensions are important to customers. But customers may make tradeoffs between the dimensions. In some situations, they may be willing to give up value in less important dimensions to get higher value in another, more important one. Remember, although the tangible dimension is the least important dimension, it's the first one customers encounter and see. Thus, influencing their first impression of the company.

Factors influencing customer perception

Customer perceptions aren't created in a vacuum. There are factors influencing the way customers evaluate the service received and thus their perceptions (Figure 3.2). Here are a few of those factors:

- **Price** — Customers compare the service received to the price paid. They create a kind of a value ratio. High ratio means high perception and satisfaction and vice versa for low ratio. The higher the price for the same level of quality service, the lower the ratio and thus the lower the value and perception of that service. The opposite happens for a lower price paid for the same level of service quality.
- **Service recovery** — Customers want to have insurance on their purchase. Any purchase. Companies that take responsibility and

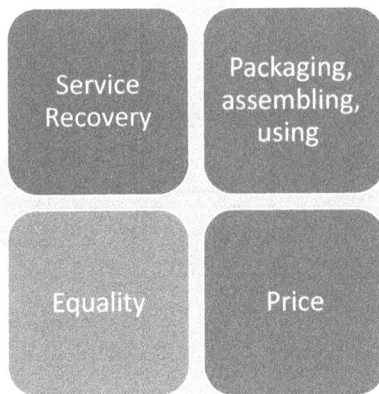

Figure 3.2. Factors Influencing Customer Perception

recover from failures get higher customer perception. The first question a customer asks after deciding to purchase a product or service is: "What will happen if something goes wrong with the product/service bought?" An answer, "We just sell the product. You will have to call the importer and talk to them," leads to a lower perception of the service. An answer of "We will replace it right away, no questions asked," leads to a higher perception.

- **Packaging, assembling, using** — The simplicity and convenience in unboxing, initial installation, and usage of the product or service influences perception. The easier it's to install and use, the higher the perception. Complexity, difficulty, and wasted time leads to frustration and much lower perception of the experience.

- **Equality** — Customers expect to receive the same level of service other customers like them receive. When they hear other customers got a better deal or a better treatment, the perception of the service received will be lower.

Conclusion

For every encounter that customers have with a company, expectations are formed, a journey is taken, and an evaluation of the encounter occurs. Every evaluation can be placed on a continuum from positive to negative. On the positive end, customers are happy and delighted with the encounter. On the negative end, customers are dissatisfied and frustrated with the encounter. The place on the continuum is determined by a comparison between what they expected to get and what they perceived they actually got. Consequently, understanding customers' expectations and perceptions is fundamental to understanding experiences.

In a digital, connected world, customers' expectations for what constitutes an acceptable or even exceptional experience keep rising. They challenge companies to keep up. They require companies to design a system that can fulfill those higher expectations and generate experiences in a precise, logical, flawless way, balancing automation and human interactions.

References

[1] Hyken, S. (2018). What Customers Want And Expect. Available at https://www.forbes.com/sites/shephyken/2018/08/05/what-customers-want-and-expect/?sh=47030e177701

[2] Maechler, N., Neher, K., and Park, R (2016). From touchpoints to journeys: Seeing the world as customers do. Available at https://www.mckinsey.com/business-functions/marketing-and-sales/our-insights/from-touchpoints-to-journeys-seeing-the-world-as-customers-do

[3] McKinsey & Company (2017). Customer Experience: New capabilities, New Audiences, New Opportunities (Number 2, June). Available at https://www.mckinsey.de/~/media/mckinsey/industries/public%20and%20social%20sector/our%20insights/cx%20compendium%202017/customer-experience-compendium-july-2017.pdf

[4] Salesforce (2021). How Are Customer Touch Points Changing? Available at https://www.salesforce.com/research/customer-touch-points/

[5] Aussant, P. (2022). Top 35+ Customer Experience Statistics to Know in 2022. Available at https://astutesolutions.com/blog/articles/customer-experience-statistics

[6] Retail Customer Experience.com (2018). Survey: Consumers want Amazon-like Store Experience. Available at https://www.retailcustomerexperience.com/news/survey-consumers-want-amazon-like-store-experience/

[7] Parasuraman, A., Berry, L.L., and Zeithaml, V.A. (1991). Refinement and Reassessment of the SERVQUAL scale, Vol. 67(4). Available at https://www.researchgate.net/profile/Valarie_Zeithaml/publication/304344168_Refinement_and_reassessment_of_the_SERVQUAL_scale/links/5919b21eaca2722d7cfe633d/Refinement-and-reassessment-of-the-SERVQUAL-scale.pdf

[8] Marketing Sherpa, (2020). Understanding What Customers Want. Available at https://www.marketingsherpa.com/article/case-study/understanding-what-customers-want-5-mini-case-studies

Part 2

Design a System-Generating Xperience

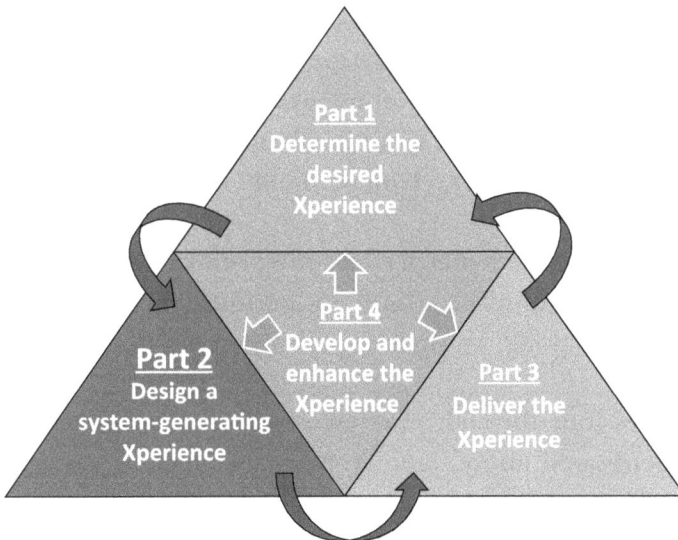

The 4D Xperience Model

Two underlying truths exist about customer experience:

1. It's a relatively simple concept to grasp.
2. It's one of the most complex to implement and accomplish.

The service environment is dynamic and convoluted. People within the company (managers and employees) interact with diverse customers who have an array of needs, in a variety of channels (Chat, phone, WhatsApp, email, etc.) They deal with and work toward solving a multitude of issues and problems. In such an environment, constructing great experiences is a challenge.

Delivering experiences doesn't happen by chance. It must be planned. The first step is to design the experience. Make sure it's consistently delivered over time, across departments and functions. Getting the whole organizational to buy-in, work in harmony, and adhere to a customer-centric ethos. Not in words, but in the thinking, planning, and daily actions of everyone in the company.

The customer-centric ethos is about having cross-functional collaboration and synergy both internally and externally, making each part of the organizational system customer-centric. Every organization consists of the same elements: Vision and strategy, culture, structure and processes, technology, management and human resources. The question is: What do all these elements focus on? To deliver experiences, each element should focus on creating value for customers.

When all the elements are customer-centric and deliver value, the system operates like a symphony, permitting people the opportunity to play along in rhythm and harmony and deliver great experiences.

Lectures four through nine take each of the organization elements mentioned above, and show what it means to make them customer-focused.

Lecture 4

Customer-First Vision & Strategy

A known Chinese proverb says "Even a journey of a thousand miles begins with a single step." People often know this part of the proverb. Many of them don't know that this proverb includes another sentence. That sentence is "That single, first step has to be in the right direction!"

The proverb should coincide with the company's vision and strategy. The vision is the end goal of a thousand miles journey. The strategy sets the first step in the right direction. Vision and strategy guide everyone in the company. At every thought, decision, action, behavior, or uncertain situation, the two are intertwined and can't be separated.

To create great experiences, the vision and strategy have to put customers first and value creation at the core of the company.

Customer-First Vision (CFV)

A vision is the ultimate goal, the audacious dream that the company declares it wants to achieve in the distant future. At first glance, it seems outrageous and feels unreachable. But that is exactly the point. The vision requires people to dream and believe what the company will be when it "grows up." It's important not to confuse the vision statement with the mission statement. While the vision is why the company exists and dreams of being, the mission statement is about what people have to do to advance the vision.

An effective CFV is composed of a few words or a sentence. It states the experience or value proposition that the company aspires to provide to its customers. It's clear, simple to understand, exciting, and creates an emotional connection and a common purpose for everyone to follow. Each employee knows the vision by heart and understands how they contribute toward achieving it. Managers know what to do to advance the vision. The company can measure its progress toward achieving the vision.

An effective CFV achieves three major goals:

1   Unifies everyone around a specific organizational identity and a common goal.
2   Makes people feel part of something bigger and meaningful than just their job and daily assignments.
3   Inspires and motivates people to be the best at what they do.

Here is a list of companies from different industries with a customer-first vision:

Company	The Vision
Amazon	Earth's most customer-centric company.
Workday	Put people at the center of enterprise software.
Adobe	Move the web forward and give web designers and developers the best tools and services in the world.
Nordstrom	Give customers the most compelling shopping experience possible.
Zappos	Delivering happiness to customers, employees, vendors.
Jet Blue	Inspire humanity — both in the air and on the ground.

(Continued)

Company	The Vision
Cleveland Clinic	To be the best place for care anywhere and the best place to work at healthcare
Philips	Improving people's lives through meaningful innovation.
Hyatt	Provide authentic hospitality by making a difference in the lives of the people we touch every day.
Trip Advisor	Help people around the world plan and have the perfect trip.
Nike	Bring inspiration and innovation to every athlete in the world. If you have a body, you are an athlete.
Paypal	Build the web's most convenient, secure, cost-effective payment solution.
Hubspot	Make the world inbound. We want to transform how organizations attract, engage, and delight their customers.
Charles Schwab	Helping investors help themselves.
Ikea	Create a better everyday life for many people.
Harley-Davidson	Fulfill dreams through the experience of motorcycling.
Norfolk Southern	Be the safest, most customer-focused and successful transportation company in the world.
Shopify	Make commerce better for everyone, so businesses can focus on what they do best: building and selling their products.
Bulletproof	Help people perform better, think faster, and live better.

To check the vision strength and how imbedded it is in people, simply asking people to state it will do. Being able to state the vision, even if it isn't word for word, means it's probably part of their daily actions and guides them in their work. If they don't remember it, then the vision is meaningless.

The strength of the CFV is tested in a time of crisis. When an economic debacle hits, revenues often fall. To counter that trend, executives start cost-cutting initiatives. The highest cost is usually slashed first. That means service providers and perks for customers. In other words, the quality of service and experience is compromised. When that happens, people realize that the vision is just words and only important when things are going well, automatically making the CFV hollow.

In contrast, when the company continues to provide great experiences in a time of crisis, it strengthens the customer-first vision and employees' trust in the company. Employees' commitment to delivering experiences is boosted and their belief in their work and serving customers, surges. Customers receive the same level of care and know that no matter what, they can count on the company to keep its promises. This leads to higher commitment and loyalty, reducing marketing and sales cost needed to attract new customers.

Once a customer-first vision is set, the next step is turning the words in the vison to actions and that is done by designing a customer-first strategy.

Customer-First Strategy (CFS)

Does a company really need a strategy to send a technician to fix a problem in a customer's home or for a service representative to answer a call in a professional and caring way? The answer is probably no. CFS isn't about a specific encounter. CFS is about getting everyone to deliver consistently, over time, upon the company's standard level of experience.

A customer-first strategy (CFS) is the formula or game plan that guides the people in the company on the journey to bring the words of the customer-first vision to life. It systematically helps people make decisions and take actions needed to meet and exceed customer expectations. Without such a strategy, people choose their own subjective path and the result is inconsistent and often ineffective service that leads to frustrated customers.

CFS places customers at the center, having their best interest at heart and making great experiences part of the company's DNA. This means getting everyone to constantly think about serving customers, listening to them and speaking their language. Regardless of the person's rank, department, role, or function. Experiences underpin everything, from executive decision-making to company's policies and resource allocation. Ultimately, this defines what the company is and how customers are treated throughout the relationship cycle, from the moment potential customers first interact with the company to the point they decide to churn.

> A Good Example — Amazon
> The company places the customer front and center by having an empty chair in every executive meeting. That chair belongs to the customer. Every decision has to pass the ultimate question "What would the customer say about that?" Given that Amazon's vision is "To be earth's most customer-centric company", if any decision doesn't create value for customers, then it's not worth making. That mentality trickles down through the ranks and eventually turns into a great individual service performance.

Developing CFS

Customers reach out to companies and buy things because they have to get something done. They have a "job" to do. The company has to figure out what each customer's job is and develop the capabilities across the company to offer the best possible solution delivered in the most convenient way. This creates a value proposition that customers love and keeps them coming back again and again.

Great value can be delivered only when the system, people, and technology are in sync, striving for excellence, and being unique. Not by "playing defense" and matching what competitors are doing, but by aligning internal business priorities and coordinating many different functions, skills, and practices needed to set the right experience standard. Appointing a senior executive to be in charge of orchestrating and driving service execution and ensuring service excellence is adopted across the organization.

In developing the strategy, the following questions should be answered:

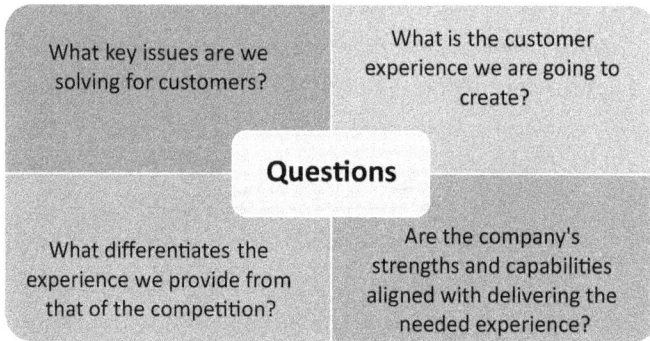

What key issues are we solving for customers?	What is the customer experience we are going to create?
Questions	
What differentiates the experience we provide from that of the competition?	Are the company's strengths and capabilities aligned with delivering the needed experience?

The answers help clear what customers need, what the company can distinctively do well, and what customer experience should look like. This allows the creation of a standardized experience and service best practices that people in the company can adopt and execute.

Delivering a great experience requires a commitment from every part of the organization. Everyone has to agree on what the company represents and then follow suit:

- Every department embraces the organizational strategy and executes it by delivering experiences to customers (whether external or internal) on every interaction.
- Every person has the knowledge, skills, and abilities to deliver a great experience. Each person knows their role, what their responsibilities are, and how they can deliver upon the strategy.
- Every decision and action has to create value and enhance the customer experience; if it doesn't, it stops immediately. Always.

When everyone in the company consistently delivers on what customers need and expect through the company's products and services, it means the strategy is effective and successful. Over time, constant adjustment should be made to the strategy, fitting the dynamic business environment and changes in customers' needs and preferences. Constant adjustment eliminates the need to make a dramatic overhaul which is rarely effective. A radical change often leads to disorder and confusion in which people struggle to deliver great experiences. Keeping the core strategy and making adjustments helps preserve the experiences, creates calmness, and sends a message to both employees and customers that the organization is reliable.

Apple mastered the CFS by delivering an intuitive and productive experience. Everything Apple does reinforces its CFS. Stores are spacious, open, and customers can use the products to feel, see and realize if there is a fit to their needs. Its website is sleek, simple, and easy for customers to get what they need. The company's service people are knowledgeable and savvy, providing professional answers without wasting customer's time. Apple refuses to compromise — even when its sales slowed in fiscal year 2016. The company never cut on customers' perks and level of experience. Apple's cultish fan base is a testimony to the emotional connection it builds by consistently delivering on its value proposition.

A Good Example — Cleveland Clinic

The company built its CFS by working backward. The company began with an "unrealistic" goal that will greatly benefit customers and then went to work figuring out how it could be achieved. The goal? Anybody calling the Cleveland Clinic for an appointment, with any specialty, would be seen that same day. Cleveland Clinic's success in pulling this off is quite an accomplishment when considering it's in contrast to the month-long waits that some specialists demand their patients to endure [2].

This commitment to speed comes in part from Cleveland Clinic's awareness of the growing number of millennial patients it sees and whom it expects to see more of as they age and start families of their own. Nobody of any age wants to wait, but expectations of the millennial generation are especially accelerated, and the company has to think today what it will have to do in the future.

Objectives of CFS

A successful CFS takes customers' expectations and translates that information into best practices that enable the delivery of great experiences, as Figure 4.1 demonstrates.

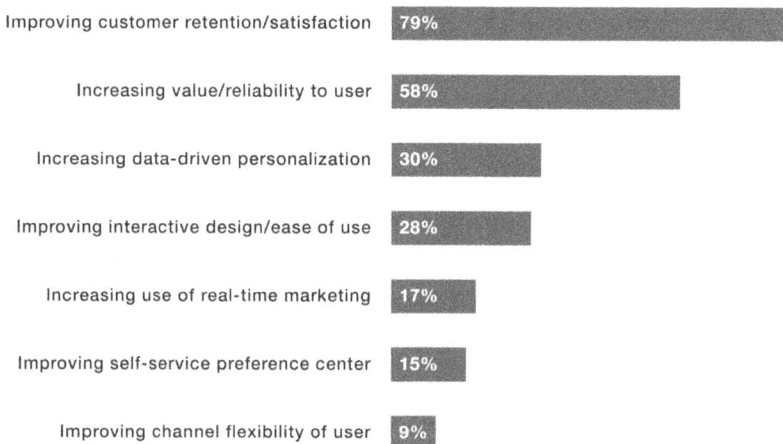

Improving customer retention/satisfaction	79%
Increasing value/reliability to user	58%
Increasing data-driven personalization	30%
Improving interactive design/ease of use	28%
Increasing use of real-time marketing	17%
Improving self-service preference center	15%
Improving channel flexibility of user	9%

Figure 4.1.   The Primary Objectives of a Customer Experience Strategy

Source: https://www.digitalmarketingcommunity.com/researches/strategies-tactics-and-trends-for-customer-experience-report-2019-ascend2/

A successful CFS helps reach the following objectives (see Figure 4.2 on the next page):

Build trust — Establish confidence with customers by implementing activities and processes that boost customers' trustworthiness in the company. Those can range from making sure promises are kept, to embracing actions that show

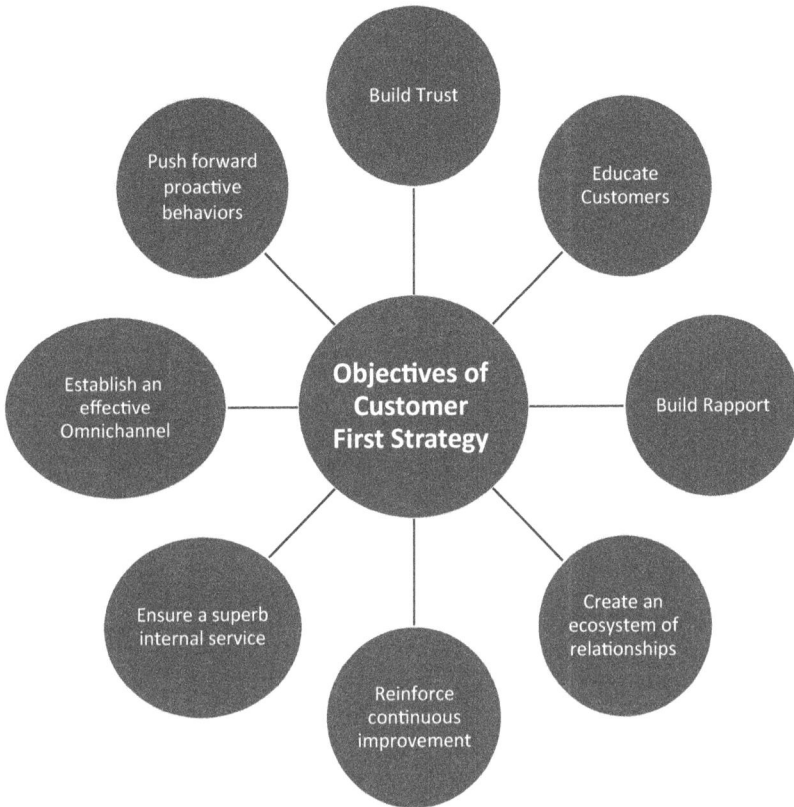

Figure 4.2. Objectives of Customer-First Strategy

transparency and communicate effectively, all the way to taking initiatives that benefit customers.

Build rapport — Focus on constructing long-term rapport with customers rather than short-term transactions. Make sure relationships with customers are constantly developed and loyalty-related actions are taken. Get to intimately know each and every customer and personalize the interactions with them.

Create an ecosystem of relationships — Establish unity with everyone — suppliers, distributors, industry associations, institutional partners, and government agencies. With such networks of relationships, the company can provide customers more options, more information, and become more efficient in getting them what they want.

Push forward proactive behaviors — Get everyone to take initiatives. Look for ways to help customers without being asked to do so; make them an offer that better suits their usage or behavior; fix a problem before customers even notice it; send them information that they once asked for and is now available.

Educate customers — Help customers optimize the usage of products and services purchased. Make sure customers are adequately taught and trained to do things the right way; Show them the company has their best interests at heart.

Establish an effective Omnichannel — Deliver seamless experiences consistently across all touch points, including brick-and-mortar, online, phone, kiosks, and mobile; smartly offer channels according to customer expectations and cost-to-serve; eliminate the division between offline and online; make the interaction through an App feel the same as face-to-face; allow customers to hop between channels; for example, they start the interaction in one channel (a website or mobile apps) and finish it in another channel (phone or a retail store).

Ensure a superb internal service — The quality of service between people and departments inside the company, significantly impacts the quality of experience for external customers. If employees get a poor service from within, why would they want to provide a great experience externally? Internal service and external service are "joined at the hip." The strategy has to look at them together rather than as separate initiatives. Ensuring that seamless interactions occur between departments, backroom-front line, and headquarters-field.

Reinforce continuous improvement — People, processes, and systems can always be improved and get better. The strategy has to establish a "continuous improvement mentality" among people, encouraging them to identify opportunities to do things better.

Establishing a dynamic CFS

As organizations grow, rules and regulations are added and the system becomes more complex. Many organizations have reached a point at which bureaucracy and red tape become the norm and employees waste their time and effort "fighting" the system. In a dynamic business environment that exists today, a complex system is a major hurdle in delivering experience. A more agile system is required for success. A system that is built according to three pillars — simpler, easier, convenient (SEC) (Figure 4.3). It's a system that allows employees the flexibility and space needed to respond quickly to customers' needs and freely manage challenges that appear during encounters.

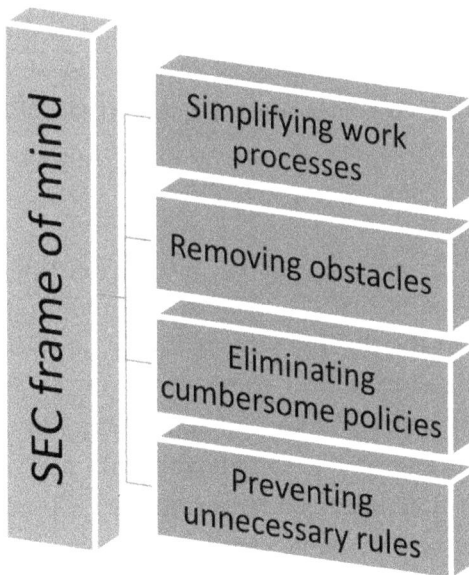

Figure 4.3.   SEC — Simple, Easy, Convenient

How SEC can the system get? Nordstrom, the successful retailer, has an employee handbook that starts with this introduction: "We're glad to have you with our company. Our number one goal is to provide outstanding customer service. Set both your personal and professional goals high. We have great confidence in your ability to achieve them." It follows by one paragraph with one rule: "Use good judgment in all situations." It ends with the following statement: "If you have a question, feel free to ask your supervisor."[3]. As the company grew, it added more guidelines, but none of them restrict Rule #1. There is no greater flexibility or way to give employees the opportunity to take action, do what has to be done, and provide a special customer experience.

A simple system is an efficient system that enables employees to save time and energy in doing what's needed. Such a system has fewer errors and less time and effort have to be spent on redoing the work as well as compensating customers for those mistakes.

Every aspect of the strategy should go through a simple test: "If it makes employees' lives or customers' lives simpler and better, then continue with the chosen way. Otherwise, stop and choose a different path." There are no ifs, ands, or buts. It's black or white, yes or no. Once thinking SEC becomes a habit, it simplifies managers', employees', and customers' lives, thus benefiting everyone.

Conclusion

A successful customer-first vision and customer-first strategy intertwine to articulate the distinctive experience and value proposition the company wishes to deliver to its customers. They set the foundation for the service delivery, balancing the sometimes-in-opposition requirements of long-term goals and objectives with specific short-term actions and behaviors. It keeps the system agile enough to adapt to a dynamic environment while allowing people to go "full speed ahead" in serving customers.

References

[1] Fontanella, C. (2022). 9 Customer Experience Trends & Stats That'll Define the Next Year. Available at https://blog.hubspot.com/service/customer-experience-trends

[2] Solomon, M, (2016). The Heart of Hospitality. Select books Inc. NewYork, NewYork.

[3] Kahn, H. (2016). How Nordstrom Made Its Brand Synonymous with Customer Service (and How You Can Too). Available at https://www.shopify.com/retail/119531651-how-nordstrom-made-its-brand-synonymous-with-customer-service-and-how-you-can-too

Lecture 5

A Customer-Obsessed Culture

"How do you stay ahead of ever-rising customer expectations? There's no single way to do it — it's a combination of many things. But building a culture that puts customers first and sets high standards, is certainly a big part of it."

Jeff Bezos

A customer-obsessed culture (COC) is a set of values that determines the mindset, beliefs, and behaviors of all the company's layers — from the board of directors to senior executives, managers, all the way to employees. Only when everyone in the organization believes that "customers come first" and embraces this belief, that delivering great experiences is possible.

While the vision is the ultimate goal and the strategy is the path to achieve the goal, culture is the compass, the map and road-signs that ensure people follow the path and stay on course. No matter how clear the customer-first strategy was set, people won't consistently execute it and make the right decisions without a culture that supports and guides them. In other words, the culture is the framework that pilots everyone all the way towards delivering desired experiences.

Herb Kelleher, the legendary CEO of Southwest Airlines, said "Culture is what people do when no one is looking." The culture is a reflection of the organization. When behaviors and actions at the leadership level and policies and processes at the operations level are customer-focused and service-oriented, then a COC is created. People embrace it and act accordingly. In contrast, if those behaviors and actions focus on something else, then the culture isn't customer-centric.

The culture doesn't just influence employees, it also influences customers. Upon receiving the service, they are exposed to the norms, behaviors and attitude that exist in the company. As customers, we all know it. Upon entering a company, we look around and watch what people do, their body language, and how they interact with other customers. That observation often tells us how much people care about providing quality service and helping customers. If nobody smiles, employees seem tired and unmotivated, and the place is a mess, we aren't surprised when the experience received is poor. The company's culture and the executives-managers-employees relationship is reflected in employees' treatment of customers. There is no way to hide it. This is why a customer-obsessed culture is a key ingredient in cementing a competitive advantage and achieving long-term success.

Effective customer-obsessed culture leads to service-oriented habits, attitude, and practices that result in higher service performance. To understand what a COC is, let's look at its different components, starting with the objectives.

Objectives of a Customer-Obsessed Culture

A successful COC motivates everyone to take responsibility and do whatever is needed to make the customer happy. People feel inspired when everyone in the company is working together, adhering to the same values. A strong COC enables the company to reach several important objectives (see Figure 5.1 on the next page):

1. **Create a customer experience identity** — By putting customers first and devoting considerable amount of money, time, and

Figure 5.1. Objectives of a Customer-Obsessed Culture

effort toward delivering great experiences, the culture ensures a customer-obsessed identity. Over time, the identity becomes a rich source of individual and organizational pride.

2. **Promote collaboration** — When everyone in the company works together to deliver great experiences, conflict is mitigated, and it's easier to collaborate and work in harmony. The internal service experience is outstanding, everything flows with minimal obstacles, which ultimately makes it easier to serve customers.

3. **Set excellence as a standard** — Great experiences require a standard of excellence. Good isn't good enough. The company's culture ensures that the excellence standards set by the strategy are taught to everyone and they comply. This inspires people to go above and beyond customers' expectations.

4. **Achieve consistency** — When every department and every person in the company adhere to the same values and behave accordingly, consistent high quality service can be delivered across the company.

5. **Supervise people** — The culture creates a framework that people in the company operate within. It replaces rules and regulations in monitoring people and supervising them. People who follow the culture values to a tee while doing their job, stay the course. They make the right judgement calls and take the right actions. And when they do occasionally stray off the values, colleagues stop them and bring them back to the cultural framework; hence the supervision.

6. **Attract the right customers** — A culture creates a certain vibe in the company that becomes visible to customers who visit.

Customers who like the culture will want to associate themselves with the company and come back. Other customers who have a different set of values, won't. Returning customers would also recommend the company to their friends who probably have similar values, helping the company attract the right customers.

To achieve these objectives, the right core values have to be determined and then ingrained into the company.

Determining Customer-Obsessed Core Values

A culture is composed of several core values that become part of the company's DNA and set the climate and standards of the workplace. They drive everything the company does, define what is important, and guides people on how they should behave and act at all times. When that isn't the case, core values are just empty and futile slogans.

There is no predetermined list of values that fits every company or ensures it can deliver great experiences. Each company has to determine the values that are the best fit for its circumstances, people, and customers. The values have to channel the company's greatest strengths, ideal behaviors, desired skills and best actions. These are values that are powerful, timeless, and sustainable.

Each value has to represent at least one concept that is needed to deliver great experience. Values are established as a guidepost to see the organization through both calm and rough waters. These values have to fit the company today and twenty years from now. Thus, people can unequivocally uphold the value in the face of obstacles, pressure, and economic downturn.

Values are usually a word or a phrase. One-word values can be something like transparency, professionalism, collaboration, and comfort. Easy to remember. However, to be effective that word should trigger the right emotional response from employees. Using a phrase as a core value becomes an expression that people remember. A phrase-value could be something like Zappos' "Deliver WOW through service", "Encourage wild ideas", GoDaddy's "Work fearlessly", "Be extraordinary" and "Join forces", and Hubspot's "Long-term solutions for customers".

Whether it's a word or a phrase, it's insignificant without a context that outlines the behaviors and actions associated with it. The context is often a short, one-paragraph description translating what the value means. The description should be simple and crystal-clear for employees so they can understand and act accordingly. It can include examples and even images that adequately represent the value. The better and clearer the context, the more powerful the value becomes.

Companies can't have an unlimited number of core values. The goal is to come up with a concise and short list of the right values. Choosing too few values won't capture all of the desired behaviors and unique dimensions of the organization and the experience expected to be delivered. Choosing too many values and employees might be overwhelmed, won't memorize or internalize them and as a result, the culture impact will be muted. While the number of core values differs between organizations, it usually ranges between three and five. There are successful companies that have more than five values. But they are the exception not the norm.

A COC isn't created just because it's important, or executives want it. The culture is created when the values are implemented in the company and turned from words into actions and behaviors that are internalized by employees. It's one thing to establish a set of core values; it's quite another to actualize it throughout the organization consistently over time.

Culture and its values are like a plant. Water it for years and it grows slowly and steadily. Stop watering it for a month and it withers and eventually dies. There are a variety of ways to ingrain core values.

Ingraining Core Values

A culture is an intangible entity and its core values are just words. After the values are translated into daily actions and behaviors, the goal is to ensure everyone follows the values and consistently execute those actions and behaviors while performing their job. Always. No exceptions. No excuses.

Core values are internalized when they are homogenous across the company. When people in the company see the same actions and behaviors everywhere they look, it becomes a reality and they follow along. Different actions between departments or between executives and employees create confusion and uncertainty of what are "the right actions" leading to ineffective values and a weak culture.

Making values a reality requires discipline. But that isn't enough. Without constantly reinforcing, promoting, and educating the importance of the values, they become mere slogans and lip service. Figure 5.2 illustrates three activities that help the company's values come into existence.

Leadership embodies each value

Values are as strong as top leadership actions. Employees need to see that the culture is taken seriously by the company's leadership

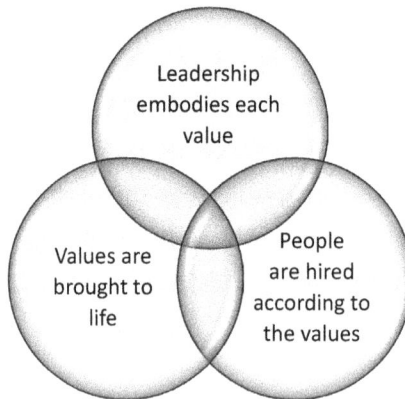

Figure 5.2. Activities to Ingrain Values

and that it isn't just some "corporate agenda" for appearance purposes. Top executives have to walk the core values and set an example for everyone to follow. When top executives live, speak, make decisions, and model their actions and behaviors according to the company's values, employees do the same and believe in the values. In other words, when executives show commitment to and passion toward the core values day-in and day-out, they become the norm for everyone and the values stick. If the leadership doesn't put the company's core values first, why would employees act any differently?

Leaders have to drive awareness of values by prioritizing the interests of the customer over other things. They should make the values part of everyone's performance reviews, sticking to them even under difficult, resources-consuming situations, rather than detracting from them when "the going gets tough."

Values are brought to life

Values become part of the company's heritage when people constantly see and hear about them. Rituals, storytelling, and symbols are tools to display the values and ingrain them in people.

Rituals — Are planned activities that emphasize the importance of values. When departments and people who exemplify the company's values are recognized, celebrated, and rewarded, their importance is paraded for everyone to see, leading other people to follow a similar path. Apple and Charles Schwab have a ritual of no commission on sales but rather on providing great experiences for customers. As a result, employees don't try to sell the most expensive product or service to customers. Rather, they look for and provide the best solution for the customer's issue at hand.

Storytelling — Are anecdotes told from one person to another and contain important lessons that highlight the company's values. Stories bring meaning to human lives and thus are a natural communication and learning tool. They are a great way to embed simple anecdotes of the company's values in people's minds. Well-told stories incorporate customer insights that articulate to employees the right behaviors and actions they need to embrace.

A well-known story is told in the department store chain, Nordstrom. It's a story that represents its legendary service through its well-known liberal, unlimited return policy that states: We will replace anything that was unjustly wornout. The story is told as follows. Many years ago a customer rolled a pair of tires into a Nordstrom store. He insisted he bought them at the store, wanted to return them according to the store policy, and asked for his money back. Nordstrom has never sold tires and the guy didn't produce any kind of a receipt. But the story is that the store manager refunded the money just to keep intact its core value of a liberal return policy.

A Good Example — Charlotte-Mecklenburg Police Department Academy

At the academy the following story is told: A suspected cop-killer murdered three police officers but spared another police officer who stopped him on a regular traffic-stop (the police officer didn't know he was wanted).

After the murderer was caught, he was interviewed and was asked why he didn't kill the police officer. The Chief of Police said that the murderer said "the Officer was so polite, respectful and professional, I couldn't do it."

Yes, your appearance and the way you treat and talk to some-one else can save your life.

Symbols — Are physical elements that represent the meaning of values. In Disney Parks, every employee carries a small card that outlines the actions that symbolize the company's core values. The company also uses movie and service-oriented language. For exam-ple, job titles (Employees are cast members and customers are guests) and actions (Fireworks are wishes and employee-orientation is called tradition). At Wendy's, the fast-food chain, the hamburgers are square-shaped in a round-shaped bun. When the founder of the chain, Dave Thomas, was asked why this is the case, he said "So every person in the company knows that we don't cut corners in making the hamburgers."

A Good Example — Zappos

The company randomly prints one of their ten values on every package shipped to customers. It highlights the importance placed on these values for employees as well as customers.

People are hired according to the values

Hiring for attitude and behaviors that fit the company's values sends a clear message about the importance of the values (Figure 5.3). Hiring people without service values weakens the customer-oriented culture and thus the organization, no matter how talented and experienced those hires might be.

The relevance of the values starts during the selection process of candidates. Interviewing in a room that has the company's core values written on the walls sends a clear message to candidates. Talking passionately about the values during the interview reinforces the message. Overall, this process attracts the candidates who fit the company's values and sends off those who don't. When a mistake happens and a candidate hired doesn't honor the values, he or she

Figure 5.3. Fit to Core Values Comes First

should be let go immediately. If the employee stays, the values are compromised, and people know it.

Strong customer-obsessed values also act like a homing beacon for talented people working in other companies. Top performers often seek out companies with strong values. They know such companies have a good working environment in which they can develop and thrive. A culture that empowers them to succeed. Those employees smoothly join the company and contribute right away, thus strengthening the values even more and enabling the company to provide even better experiences.

Consequently, to ingrain values in people's mind, heart, and every day routine, they must be constantly communicated. Not once a month or once a quarter or when crises arise, but all the time. New ways to instill the values should be used to keep people's attention and interest in the values over time. The more creative and inventive the ways in getting the message across, the better!

Characteristics of a Successful Customer-Obsessed Culture

A successful COC guides people's mindset, judgement, decision-making, and actions in every situation and encounter with customers. Such a culture is usually characterized by several aspects (see Figure 5.4 on the next page).

Helps embrace service change — Customers' needs and expectations, competitor landscape, regulations, and technology constantly transform and change. A successful culture supports people in times of change, and helps them adapt. It creates a dynamic working environment in which managers and employees embrace and accept change rather than fear it. In such a culture, people learn from mistakes and get better, rather than avoid similar situations or get punished for them.

Empowers service providers — The culture has to empower people and give them the autonomy to make decisions while interacting

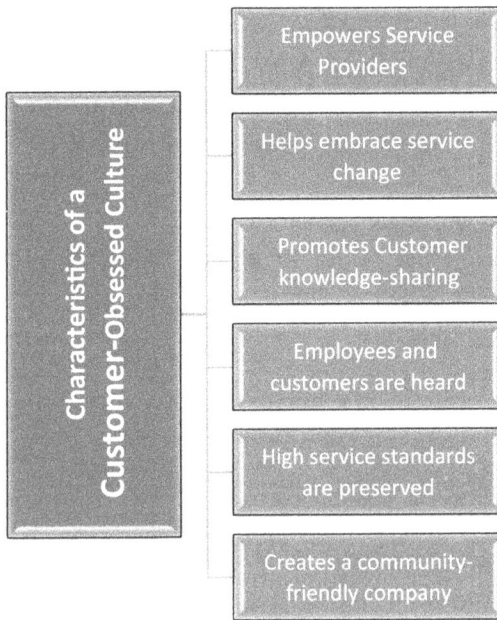

Figure 5.4. Characteristics of a Customer-obsessed Culture

with customers. The culture has to arm employees with all the tools needed to provide customers with the best solutions, satisfy their needs and WOW them when possible.

Promotes customer knowledge-sharing — Companies working in silos cause people to be isolated from important and relevant customer research and insights. Departments may work relentlessly on finding a unique solution to a problem only to learn that another department already came up with a solution to the issue. As a result, time and resources are wasted, which hurts peoples' ability to deliver the best possible experience. A successful culture eliminates this problem by making knowledge-sharing a common practice across the company.

Employees and customers are heard — Service providers interact daily with customers. This gives them unique insights and understanding of customers. They hold information no one else in the company has — what customers like, dislike, struggle with, and need. Yet, they are rarely, if ever, invited to executive meetings to speak and share their knowledge. A successful culture gives employees a voice in the board room and involves them in top executives' decision-making process. It also gets CEOs out of their luxurious offices and into the field, where they can see what is going on and talk to employees and customers. When employees are involved and see the CEO walking around, they buy into the COC and internalize the company's values.

High service standards are preserved — Every company sets high standards. But those standards tend to start high and go down over time. A COC helps keep everyone dedicated to high service standards. Adhering to high standards sends a clear message that mediocrity is unacceptable. It also entices people to exceed the standard level and do more than expected.

Creates a community-friendly company — The culture has to include social responsibility and sustainability missions and not just economic one. It shows customers and employees that the company is a "force for good" that positively influences the community. People want to be associated with companies that really care about and contribute to the community.

Conclusion

A successful customer-obsessed culture is a framework that watches over everyone and guides them all the way to delivering desired experiences. It determines their mindset, beliefs, and behaviors. It sets service excellence as the framework for people to meticulously follow and thus define the corporate character. It determines how people interact with other people, getting everyone to "live and breathe customers." It creates a competitive advantage and causes competitors to admire the company.

Building a COC isn't a once-off effort; it's an ongoing process. It requires constant promotion and maintenance, making sure people constantly follow the core values. When all is said and done, usually more is said than done. A successful customer-obsessed culture makes sure more is done. Much more.

Lecture 6

Service-Oriented Organizational Structure and Processes

"For the last 60 years we've operated command and control in a hierarchal structure. A change is needed. We need a horizontal structure in which everyone feels a collective responsibility towards the customer. We need to empower the whole organization to feel they can personalize the delivery of CX."

Dr. Jules Goddard, London Business School

The organizational structure and processes shape and direct the internal service — how the company is organized, how people interact with each other, lines of communication, and the flow of work and information. A service-oriented structure reduces obstacles, friction, and constraints to a minimum, creating a great internal service that helps people deliver great external service.

In the digital age, customers expect companies to be agile, act quickly, and make fast decisions. That is the reason why flexibility is key to organizational survival in the 21st century. The organizational structure is no exception. A dynamic environment requires an elastic structure that accommodates the customers' changing and evolving needs. A rigid or poorly designed structure leads to complexities and lack of coordination, which doesn't create the conducive environment needed to serve customers. When a dynamic environment meets a stagnant structure and poorly designed processes, the organization struggles to operate efficiently, manage effectively, and see improvements over time.

The dynamic environment has led companies to move away from the classic pyramid organizational structure and embrace new structures such as the team-based, flat lattice structures used by W.L. Gore & Associates, the democratic structure used by WD-40 Company, and the Holacracy and self-management structure used by Zappos [1].

New technologies have made it possible to make the structure more adaptable, enabling collaboration within the structure in ways that weren't possible just a few years ago. Such has resulted in improved communication and flow of information while cutting across functional and geographical silos.

This lecture outlines the different characteristics of a service-oriented structure and experience-enabling processes. Let's start with inverting the organizational pyramid.

Inverting the Organizational Pyramid

The classic pyramid structure based on hierarchy, silos, and functions is still a dominant theme in many companies. Such a structure focuses on leading the masses and running the organization in the most efficient way possible. There is a chain of command, division of labor, and everyone knows their place from top to bottom. While this structure is simple to understand and relatively easy to operate, it limits empowerment and collaboration, and doesn't do well with change. In essence, it limits the freedom and flexibility needed to engage effectively with customers and deliver desired experiences.

A service-oriented structure is characterized first and foremost by inverting the pyramid upside down (Figure 6.1 on the next page). Such a move creates several essential service-oriented changes.

Employees are on top — In the classic pyramid, employees are at the bottom of the hierarchy. They are perceived as expendable and

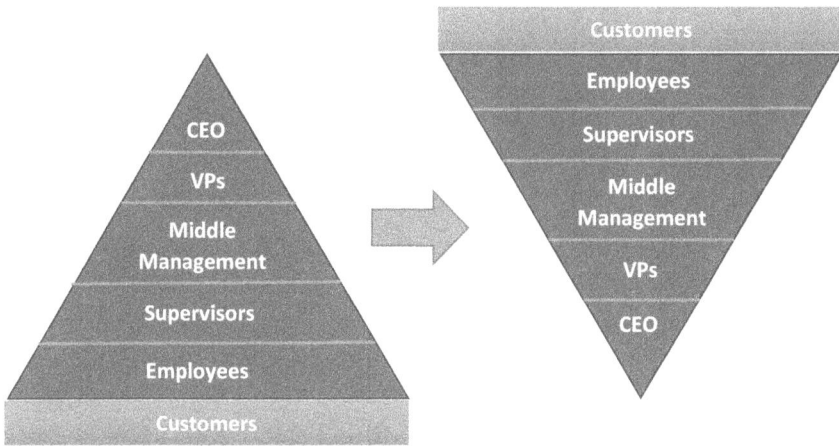

Figure 6.1. Inverting the Classic Organizational Pyramid

often receive limited attention and investment. Given that employees serve customers, this is a barricade in getting them to deliver experiences.

When employees are on top of the hierarchy, they become important. Management starts to listen to them, removes obstacles, and fixes problems that hinder their service performance.

Customers are above everyone — In the classic pyramid, employees are at the bottom and since customers are adjacent to them, their place is even below employees.

When the pyramid inverts, employees are on top and customers are placed again adjacent — but this time they are above everyone. People are looking up at customers and working toward helping them get what they need. That makes sense given that without customers, the organization ceases to exist.

The CEO is the base of the pyramid — In the classic pyramid, the CEO is on top and employees who have the least experiences, minimal power, and limited decision-making ability are the base of the company.

When the pyramid is inverted, the CEO is now the base. The person who has the most power, who is in charge of everyone, who looks at the whole system and makes the most important decisions, is the cornerstone of the company.

Executives and managers serve employees and customers — In the classic pyramid, employees serve middle managers who serve upper-level management who serves executives who in turn serve the CEO. Everyone focuses on the CEO and their executive team works accordingly.

When the pyramid is inverted, the CEO serves executives who serve upper and middle management who serve employees. Executives and managers become the coaches, instructors, and service providers for everyone in the company. The CEO is the number one service provider with one goal — help everyone be better, do better, and do more. The "me approach" of leadership changes to "we approach" in which control is deregulated, decentralized, and a substantial part is transferred to the frontline, allowing them to take initiatives and fulfill customers' needs.

After inverting the pyramid, it's important to understand several key building blocks of the organizational structure that influence the experiences delivered.

The Building Blocks of a Customer-Oriented Organizational Structure

The organizational structure has to suit its beneficiaries — managers and employees. There are several elements in the design of the structure that determine how people operate, work, and interact with customers.

Hierarchy — Is the number of layers of managers that exist between the CEO and the service providers. The more layers there are, the more bureaucracy is created which reduces flexibility. Everything takes more time. Information and decisions have to go through multiple layers of approval, slowing things down to a halt. It requires employees to jump through hoops to get things done.

This frustrates everyone, hurts performance, and reduces the quality of service.

Companies that want to deliver experiences have to flatten the structure by reducing the number of layers. Such a change makes the organization more nimble and yields the following positive result:

- Empowered service providers — With less layers, more authority and responsibility are transferred to service providers. This allows them to treat customers the right way by responding immediately to any request.
- Clearer and faster communication — With less layers, information is transferred quickly and accurately up and down the structure. This allows employees to react immediately and avoid unnecessary mistakes.
- Easier change implementation — With less layers, executives can communicate directly with service providers, making coordination and execution of changes simpler and better.
- Increasing initiatives — With less layers, there is less micromanagement. Employees can use the authority and responsibility they got to push ideas and drive innovation.

Consequently, a flat structure enables people to thrive and sets them up for success. They feel the company trusts them and in return they deliver higher achievements.

Centralization — Describes where decisions are untimely made in the organization. If decision-making power is concentrated up the ranks and there is a clear chain of command, the organizational structure is centralized. If executives push down the authority for decision-making all the way down to employees, the structure is decentralized.

According to the acclaimed study "The Iceberg of Ignorance" by Sidney Yoshida, 100% of an organization's front line problems are known by employees; 74% are known by supervisors; 9% are known by managers and only 4% are known by top management [2]. Given the findings it makes sense to empower service providers. Giving them more power, responsibility, and control. Thus, providing them with wiggle room needed to choose the best course of action in each service encounter without managerial approval. Consequently, decentralization, which leads to empowerment, improves people's effectiveness and the organization's operation efficiency (Figure 6.2).

When an issue becomes too complex, too sensitive or too costly, then it's escalated to the manager. That still means the organization is decentralized. Managers can use this situation to teach employees how to make the right decision when dealing with such complicated issues. The more issues employees can take care of, the more time managers have to prevent future problems, reduce obstacles, and improve employees' performance. A win-win situation.

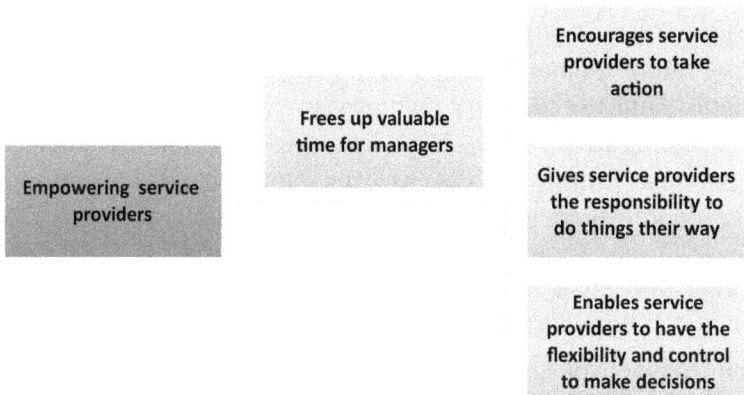

Figure 6.2.   The Effect of Empowering Service Providers

Specialization — Also known as division of labor, this is the degree to which activities or tasks in an organization are broken down and divided into many individual jobs. High specialization is beneficial as it allows people to become "masters" in specific areas, increasing their productivity as a result.

However, for delivering experiences, low specialization or a broader job, is a better fit. A broader job allows service providers to tackle an extensive array of issues that customers have. Allowing employees to become a One-Stop-Shop(OSS) for customers, taking care of all their issues from A to Z without the need to transfer them to someone else.

Customers love OSS. It's convenient, and saves them time and effort. OSS doesn't happen right away. With time, employees can broaden their capabilities by acquiring more and more knowledge and skills such as learning to professionally answer questions in different areas of expertise as finance, operations, and marketing. It's not about being an expert in each field, but knowing how to deal with the most frequently asked questions and the most typical issues.

Broadening the skillset is also beneficial for employees as they develop themselves in different fields and are exposed to different and often challenging issues. It promotes healthy learning environments which help keep employees motivated and engaged.

Formalization — Is the degree to which an employee's tasks and activities are governed by rules, policies, procedures, and other red-tape mechanisms. The goal of formalization is to set each position and keep people in-check by ensuring they do things in a certain way, time after time. This results in achieving consistency and reducing failures and mistakes to a minimum.

While formalization reduces mistakes it also reduces the degrees of freedom that service providers have and thus handcuffs them in what they can do and how they can do it when interacting with customers. A service encounter is a dynamic situation. Policies and procedures aren't built for rapid encounter, dealing with many moving parts, or personalizing actions for customers.

When employees are constantly told what to do by rules and policies, they aren't likely to be very motivated. Doing more than expected or going above and beyond for customers is out of the question.

Departmentalization (silos) — Refers to the process of dividing the organization by function (Finance, marketing, operations, service, etc.) in which each function is a department.

In organizations with rigid departmentalization, every department is a silo — highly autonomous, with limited cooperation with other departments. Every department has its own goals, rules, ways of doing things, and even a unique operating or data system. The members of each department's alliance is often firstly to the department and secondly to the company. That engenders behaviors that lead to the success of the department, but may also drive a somewhat self-centered, poor cooperation frame of mind. One department may do one thing without informing other departments that are influenced by such a move. Also, some departments might not share data and information. This could result in mistakes and wasted time, energy, and other resources — hurting the company and its customers alike.

An Interesting Fact

A good 70% of managers say silo mentality is the biggest organizational hurdle to improving customer experience [3].

Customer experiences don't fit into a silo. While silos are vertical, customers' interactions with a company are more horizontal, across silos, bouncing from the web to the call center, or from the sales department to the customer service department. Managers and employees can do their best to deliver great customer experiences within the context of their silo. The problem is, even when each group is doing their best, it can feel disconnected and broken from the customer point of view. Consequently, functional silos hamper organizational performance and contribute to inconsistent, fragmented, and ultimately frustrating experiences for customers.

Aligning the departments to focus on customers is more likely to succeed than insisting customers align themselves to each department. Breaking down the silos leads to one voice across the different channels or different departments. Customers don't have to start a new or re-explain their need any time they shift to another channel or another function. The goal is to help, not hinder, the customer from getting the necessary solution.

A Good Example — Lego

The company assembles cross-functional teams to make better decisions. This brings together people from all relevant points of view, levels, divisions, and locations.

For example, service providers become members of new product design teams, importing the voice of the customer into the process [4].

Eliminating silos improves collaboration, internal operations, and customer interaction with the company. People in one department start taking into account other department's needs and limitations. This makes it simpler to solve issues and problems, learn from each other, and advance multi-departmental, cross-functional initiatives that help the organization succeed over time.

People sometimes forget that everyone in the company works for the customer, including those who rarely communicate directly with them. Production employees, maintenance, IT, and other departments only deal with internal customers. However, through the internal interactions and service, they influence external customers.

When the building block of the organizational structure discussed above are service-oriented, it's much easier to provide great experiences. Thus, designing the right building blocks isn't nice-to-have but a must-have, for the organization to stay competitive and prosper.

A New Position: The Customer Experience Officer

The Customer Experience Officer (CXO) is a relatively new position in many companies. This is an executive position that oversees and is responsible for the company's customer experience. This position is at the same level as the CFO, CMO, and COO. Unlike these positions, the CXO position is a cross-departmental role that its goal is to nurture alignment, collaboration, and accountability for customers among everyone in the organization.

The CXO is in-charge of designing the experience and integrating it throughout the company. He or she designs a seamless customer journey and ensures that a consistent customer experience is delivered across the entire business, spanning multiple departments, units, geographies and touchpoints.

An Interesting Fact

Executives such as the COO, CMO, and CFO are <u>vertical positions</u>. They are in charge of specific disciplines (Operations, Marketing, Finance, respectively).

The CXO is more of a <u>horizontal position</u>. This position connects the multiple disciplines and achieves consensus across diverse interests in the organization. The position cuts through silos and ensures everyone focuses on customers and their experience.

The CXO role usually includes several duties and objectives:

- Assures the value proposition is consistently delivered through every service channel.
- Sparks creativity, excitement, and energy among people by listening to their ideas and suggestions for service improvement.
- Makes sure customer needs are always considered in critical decisions, organizational development, and new projects.
- Measures, tracks, and analyze customer interactions, loyalty, and brand image.
- Uses customer analytics to turn data into meaningful insights.
- Assesses and identifies gaps in the customer experience at any touchpoint across the customer journey.
- Performs a cost-benefit analysis to determine the ROI on service improvements.
- Supports service-providing employees and helps them deliver an exceptional experience.

The CXO is like a conductor of an orchestra. The conductor directs the performance of many musicians to create an incredibly impressive and cohesive piece of music. The CXO directs the performance, values, actions, and behaviors of every department and every person to create an impressive and coherent customer experience.

Customer-Oriented Processes

Processes are a chain of linked activities or steps that help get work done and deal with customers. They transform inputs into outputs, helping achieve consistency and prevent mistakes, particularly when there are safety-related or legal reasons for following rigid steps. Obviously, too many or too rigid processes that are aimed at maintaining control can get in the way of employees doing their job effectively and customers getting what they want. There is a fine line to walk in order to yield consistency but also provide the flexibility and speed needed in a service encounter.

Processes can be grouped into two major categories. First, operational processes that help create, produce, and deliver external experiences. Second, administrative processes that help run the organizational system and everything that happens internally.

Delivering high quality service requires customer-oriented and friendly processes that are experience-enablers and profit maximizers rather than employee agitators and financial loss generators (Figure 6.3).

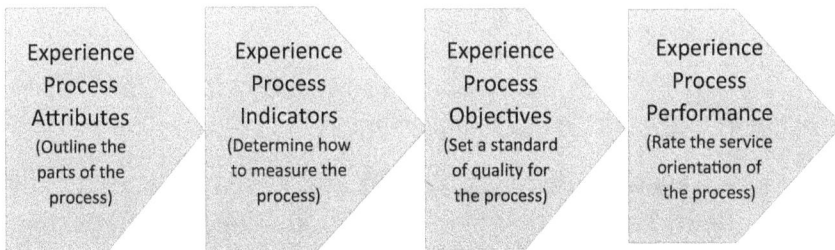

Experience Process Attributes (Outline the parts of the process)

Experience Process Indicators (Determine how to measure the process)

Experience Process Objectives (Set a standard of quality for the process)

Experience Process Performance (Rate the service orientation of the process)

Figure 6.3. Creating Experience-Enablers Processes

The outcomes of service-oriented processes

To understand if a process is service-oriented or not, two questions should be asked periodically:

1. Are customers complaining about service processes? Too slow? Too complicated? Inconvenient?
2. Are employees complaining about the processes? Too bureaucratic? Don't make sense? Makes it difficult to deliver experiences?

Service-oriented processes make the customer's life simple and convenient, improve employees' productivity, and reduce service cycle. Less time and effort are required by people to provide the desired service from first contact to resolution. This allows employees to handle more customer and not compromise on the quality of service. The organization runs smoothly with minimal waste and errors. People can focus their efforts toward serving customers rather than dealing with and even "fighting" the system.

Complex, multilayered processes lead to dysfunction, wasted resources, and undesirable performance. These ineffective and inefficient processes create bottlenecks and operational inefficiencies. As a result, people have to retake certain actions or redo parts of the work, frustrating them and reducing their motivation to serve customers. Poor experiences frustrate customers to a point that they rethink their relationship with the company. According to research, companies lose 20–30% in revenues every year due to process inefficiencies [5].

Process in a dynamic service environment

Once a process is created it's often left unchecked for years, resulting in little to no change. Any processes, no matter how effective, will stop working adequately at some point in the future as a result of the changing business environment. Processes should be modified to fit the new environment. The more time passes before a change occurs, the less effective the processes are, which increases the number of problems and failures, resulting in more errors and mistakes. People feel they are going through a muddy swamp and have to find creative ways to work around the faulty processes. This reduces morale and productivity. Everybody suffers — customers, employees, managers, and eventually the company's profits.

Many companies are unable to adapt quickly enough to the changes because process adherence is embedded in the system. Employees are extremely good at following them. Management continues to believe in the processes because they worked well in the past. Even when a change is agreed upon, small modifications are made rather than a reconstruct which is desperately needed. Companies that deliver great service prove themselves willing to abandon even good processes in order to make them exceptional. That sets them apart from their competition.

An Interesting Fact

A study shows that 53% of large organizations report outdated, overly time-consuming workflows that slow down their processes and stand in the way of customer experience evolving at the speed of the market. Companies have to rethink how teams across the organization collaborate and share information, resources and goals [6].

Improving processes

Processes should constantly be analyzed and assessed to see if they operate at peak performance. Improving processes can be incremental or a complete overhaul. Incremental improvement is best used when small scale changes are needed while the basic structure of the process is working fine. A complete overhaul is needed when too many steps in the process are broken and a new design has to be engineered. An overhaul is more difficult and scarier for people but it allows for a quantum leap rather than incremental improvement.

Improving processes isn't an easy task. People complain about a bad process but often prefer it over an unknown process. People dislike questioning things that have been done in a certain way for a very long time. They don't want to "rock the boat" or make someone feel exposed. It's often the case that the culture doesn't support change or people in the company don't realize the impact of the faulty processes. As a result, a common theme is saying that "everything is fine", keep using the ineffective processes and postponing the necessary upgrade. This hurts the customer experience and increases the burden on service providers.

Many companies have a difficult time growing because substantial amount of time and effort are spent on fixing broken processes. While fixing problems is important, it's more important to make changes in the process before it breaks down. Improving what isn't broken yet is an investment that pays itself many times over by saving resources spent unnecessarily on fixing things after they break down.

Successful companies value long-term solutions over short-term fixes. They are patient and committed to constantly improving processes, even effective ones. Each process performance and outcome from start to finish is documented in detail, showing when and where complications occurred. A more in-depth analysis also reveals why it happened. Once the company has all that information, improvements are more precise and the results are significantly better.

Conclusion

To deliver great experiences, the internal-service must first be great. Service-oriented organizational structure and customer-oriented processes are the backbone of great internal-service. Flexible and nimble enough for people to respond quickly to customer demands and provide quality service. Helping different departments and functions work seamlessly together, eliminating fragmented and compartmentalized work, improving coordination and collaboration, thus enhancing everyone's performance.

Many organizations still suffer from a misalignment between the dynamic business environment and stagnant organizational structure and processes. This leads to an inefficient organizational system. The longer organizations wait to eliminate the misalignment, the harder it's to compete and deliver great experiences.

References

[1] Swinscoe, A. (2017). How to identify the best organizational structure for your customers. Available at https://www.mycustomer.com/experience/engagement/how-to-identify-the-best-organisational-structure-for-your-customers

[2] Minnaar, J. (2018). How Real Leaders Melt the Iceberg of Ignorance With humility. Available at https://corporate-rebels.com/iceberg-of-ignorance/

[3] Shaw, C. (2013). How to Overcome Organizational Silos? Available at https://beyondphilosophy.com/how-to-overcome-organizational-silos/

[4] Scott, A. (2017). How Silos Damage Customer Experience. Available at https://www.matchboard.com.au/how-silos-damage-customer-experience/#:~:text=Each%20silo%20has%20its%20own,the%20company%20is%20simply%20incompetent

[5] Boss, J. (2016). 5 Ways Your Business Processes Could Be Hurting Your Business. Available at https://www.forbes.com/sites/jeffboss/2016/11/01/5-ways-your-business-processes-could-be-hurting-your-business/?sh=4e49cf9052e9

[6] Eubanks, M. (2020). 12 Trends for Better Digital Customer Experience in 2021. Available at https://www.fullstory.com/blog/trends-digital-customer-experience

Lecture 7

The Digital Service Transformation

"Innovation needs to be part of your culture. Customers are transforming faster than we are, and if we don't catch up, we're in trouble."

Ian Schafer, Co-Founder and CEO, Kindred

Technology is a game changer in service. It has revolutionized the way customers experience their interaction with companies. Historically, service quality was evaluated based on interactions with humans (face-to-face and phone). Over the past twenty years, the virtual world (online and self-service) has taken over the delivery of service. With advances in technology such as Artificial Intelligence, Augmented Reality, Self-service Robots, cloud computing, Apps, and social platforms, a radical, far-reaching, global service reformation is underway. The virtual world's convenience, speed, and agility are replacing humans and becoming the customers' first choice. It's a trend that is only going to intensify with the younger, digital generations growing up and the continuous opportunities that technology is opening up.

Technology is at the core of every company, playing a vital role in everything that happens. When efficient, it enhances performance; it's an experience enabler and thus a value creator. But when it's inefficient, it impairs performance and leads to frustration and dissatisfaction all around.

Successful companies see technology as an experience enabler while average companies see it as a cost reduction tool. Technology helps companies monitor, track, and measure customers' experiences, employees' conduct, and overall performance. The rich data collected helps both internally and externally. Internally, technology can quickly and accurately identify and uncover problematic or inefficient areas in the company. Externally, it can offer in-depth information and insights on every single customer, enabling the company and its people to make educated decisions that are effective in improving the customer experience.

Technology is at the center of the customer's universe. They hold smartphones in their hands and are surrounded by smart devices at home. Technology has changed the way customers interact with companies. It gives customers control over the encounter. They decide when and where to engage with the company. They can quickly do price checks and get several offers from different vendors on the spot.

Technology has positively transformed three major experience-related aspects (Figure 7.1). In the following pages the influence of technology on each of these three aspects is outlined.

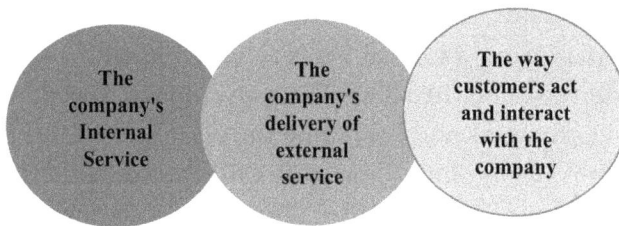

Figure 7.1. The Technology Service Delivery Transformation

Technology Transformation of the Company's Internal Service

Technology can speed up operations and make internal interactions more efficient and flawless. It offers smarter, quicker ways to do the work, reshape processes, streamline actions, and offer easy access to real-time data and support. Thus, enabling the company to fix bottlenecks, inefficiencies, or chronic systematic issues that slow down operations and inhibit important actions.

Technology can optimize the company's internal service in two major ways: Maximize people's performance and boost process efficiency.

Technology maximizes people's performance

Any person can do a better job and improve their service performance. Some can raise it "by a mile" while others can only raise it modestly. Technology enables everyone to perform better by facilitating the following outcomes (Figure 7.2).

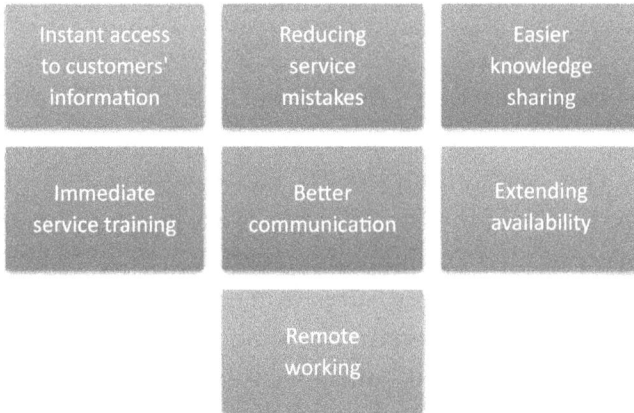

Figure 7.2.   How Technology Maximizes People's Performance

Instant access to customers' information — Cloud computing and mobile technology make it easier for any service provider to access any type of customer information quickly in real time, from their computer, at any location. No need to wait for other departments or people to provide the information. Everyone can see the history of customer interactions, and know what was said and done. This eliminates the customer's need to repeat the same information and answer the same questions, endorsing a better, quicker, and more productive interaction.

Better communication — Smartphones, internal portal systems, and social networking has brought communication to a whole new level. It has become instantaneous, collaborative, and unified. People have an easier time communicating with each other and delivering more effective messages, preventing communication gaps between departments and improving interdepartmental trust. People no longer need to be physically present to engage and communicate with other people. Virtual meetings can be done through multiple offices without having to worry about logistics. This allows everyone to be on the same page and rapidly exchange ideas and updates.

Easier knowledge sharing — An Intranet or cloud computing system ensures distribution of knowledge between departments and branches, and among employees. Those systems embed all the knowledge that people have, allowing everyone to share and learn from it. Successful service initiatives, positive actions, as well as creative solutions done in one department or branch are shared, duplicated, and implemented in other departments and branches. When knowledge is shared, efficiency is boosted, and wasted effort is substantially reduced.

Immediate service training — Educational and learning softwares can teach employees missing service skills and abilities at their desk during off-peak working hours. Simple, easy, and provided immediately. The tutorial can be short for a simple matter, or more prolonged course for more advanced skills and abilities. Technology closely monitors the learning process and tests its effectiveness through case studies.

Extending availability — With WhatsApp and other social networks, people's availability to serve customers is extensive. Technology enables people to have one phone number that simultaneously rings no matter where the customer calls to. This greatly increases the availability of the service providers, reaching them on the first try. Technology also helps service providers take care of customers wherever they are — on the go, in the office, or at home.

Reducing service mistakes — By using sensors, ID badges with built-in biometrics, GPS tracking, video cameras and wristbands, companies can follow every service encounter and analyze the interaction between customers and technology. They can understand what is done right and where mistakes are made. Technology can monitor service providers and prevent them from making mistakes by offering them real time guidance on the best course of action. Reducing the number of mistakes makes everyone happy.

Remote working — Technology has created a modern workplace in which coming to an office and working closely with colleagues in one location is no longer necessary. More and more people are working from remote locations. Advanced teleconferencing systems free people from being in one location and dealing with many tiresome logistics. They can keep their daily calendar, stay interconnected with their team, have face-to-face meetings, and stay in touch with their manager. Technology also helps managers supervise employees in remote locations. This ensures that tasks don't get off-track and deadlines aren't missed, which can potentially put projects in jeopardy and hurt performance.

Technology optimizes service processes

Process optimization refers to the practice of constantly improving workflows to a point that they work flawlessly and require minimum effort. The goal is to take out the slowness, complexity, defective and useless aspects of the process. This can be done by eliminating a step, adding a step, or upgrading an existing step in the process. By phasing out problems, the process becomes better, faster, and has less friction and time wastage. This helps service providers do a better job and deliver higher quality service.

Technology opens a whole different level of optimization. Instead of incremental process changes, leaps and bounds are possible upon reinventing the process. The transformation happens in four major ways (Figure 7.3).

Digitizing — Technology turns analog and physical service processes into digital. It simplifies the processes and makes them easier, convenient, and effortless to use. Examples: buying from physical stores, to online shopping; depositing a check in a bank's branch, to depositing it through the smartphone; paying for parking in a machine, to paying through an App on the phone.

Streamlining — Technology ensures people complete the processes as consistently as possible. Every person is different and operates in

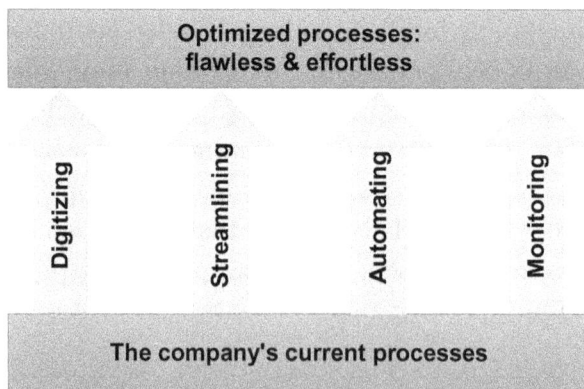

Figure 7.3. Technology Optimizes Service Processes

their own way. Forcing everyone physically to go through the same strict procedure is next to impossible. Technology makes sure it happens and people complete every step of the process in the right order, every time, at any location. Building repetition and consistency creates familiarity which gives people certainty and calmness. It's also ideal for facilitating optimal workflow, reducing mistakes to a minimum and preventing unfinished tasks.

Familiarity with the processes allows people to use them more efficiently. It lets them get what they need quickly and accurately. The more the process is used, the more the system learns how employees and customers use it and how it can be improved. Furthermore, the system remembers the typed-in information and over time can fill that information by itself, saving time.

Automating — The automation theme is simple: If a robot can do it, then a robot should do it. Repetitive tasks, grunt work, mundane assignments that require manual labor, compliance work, and especially things that require paperwork should be automated. Technology does these tasks better, faster, and more accurately; it doesn't get tired or frustrated, and thus boosts process efficiency. When manual labor is reduced to a minimum, there are less errors, things are done on time, and the flow of data is improved. People can spend more quality time with customers and focus on value-added tasks as well as higher-priority work.

Take for example, employees' onboarding process. That process requires many steps and endless paperwork which often lead new employees to commit missteps and encounter issues that negatively affect their perception of the company and even their satisfaction. Automation ensures smooth transition from one task to the next, keeps relevant people in the loop, and makes the status of the process visible. Without technology these processes become quite chaotic with mistakes and problems occurring on a regular basis.

The same can be done with processes used by customers. Going physically to the supermarket looks like this: Take a cart, put groceries in, go to a cashier whether in person or self-checkout, take the products out, scan, and bag them. Automate the process like

Amazon Go — Scan your phone at the entrance to the store, put the groceries in your bag, and just leave the store. Machines follow customers, know what they put in the bag, and the App adds up the total, uses virtual payment, and sends a receipt to the customer's WhatsApp. Everything is automated.

Monitoring — Technology is far better at monitoring and analyzing workflow than any manual way that exists. It can observe every aspect of every process from start to finish, all the time. It can measure the efficiency of the process and find miscues and problems that exist. It can show the gap between every process as is and as it should ideally be, allowing the company to better manage and improve it by making the right adjustments or modifications.

Consequently, digitizing, streamlining, automating, and monitoring the company processes yield the following positive outcomes:

- **Increased value for customers** — Minimal effort and maximum convenience
- **Improved employee satisfaction** — Focusing on important tasks that require their set of skills and avoiding robotic, Sisyphean, agitating tasks
- **Minimized miscues** — Avoiding missteps, blunders, and failures
- **Better flow** — Things go smoother from one person to another with no wait or negative surprises

By improving the internal service, technology saves the company time, money, and effort on one hand and people's frustration and dissatisfaction on the other. This improves everyone's productivity and the company's results.

Technology Transformation of the Company's Delivery of External Service

Technology tore down two fundamental barriers to service delivery: time and place. Time — service can now be provided 24/7/365.

Specific opening hours, closed dates or any other restrictions are irrelevant. Place — there are no boundaries. Customers can receive service around the globe. It can be on a remote island where the customer is vacationing, at his or her home, or on the road while driving.

Technology has changed the customer journey. Customers can get almost everything they need with ease and simplicity online without physically going anywhere or talking to anyone. Even a visit to the doctor or a personal trainer. Technology has widened the number of service platforms and channels (Social media, live chat, video and more) that customers can use.

Technology has changed the way information is collected on customers, enabling the company to track and manage every step the customer makes. The digital footprint customers leave in their virtual journey allows the collection of big data from multiple sources, formats, and forms and using it in ways never done before. Through data mining and actionable analytics, the rich data is turned into meaningful insights on how customers think, operate, and act. This enables companies to achieve closeness to customers never possible before, a closeness that yields better interactions.

Beyond the changes above, technology has transformed the external service delivery in several major ways (see Figure 7.4 on the next page).

Offer unlimited choices and infinite information — Technology helps companies open up the world of choices and information. Customers no longer have to stick with local or even national products that might not provide the necessary solution. They can see products from around the globe. Customers also have access to tremendous amount of information about what they need, options available, and opinions of people that used each option. Technology helps customers browse efficiently through the endless choices and information by offering effective search engines and recommended options based on in-depth analysis of what hundreds and thousands of other customers did in similar situations.

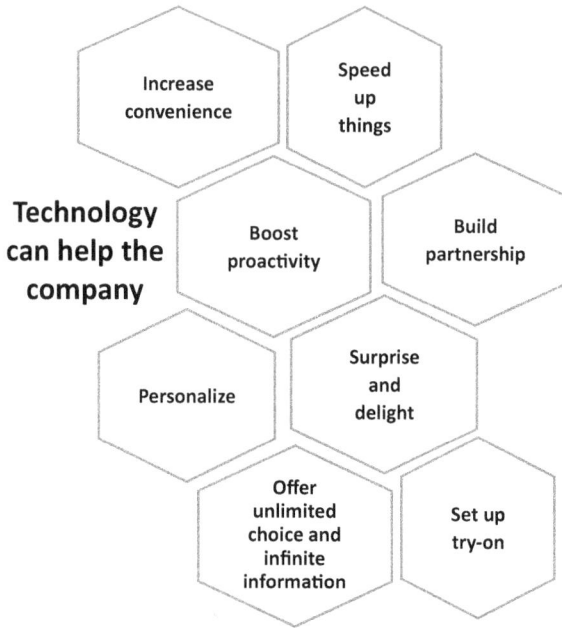

Figure 7.4. Technology Improvement of The External Service Delivery

Increase convenience — Effective technology offers customers hustle-free interaction. Through browsing, swiping, and clicking whenever they decide. No queue, no waiting. Customers calling a company can choose not to wait on hold and instead press a button on their smartphone and receive a callback when the agent is free. Customers can order drinks and food through an App, know how long it will take, and pick up the order without standing in line. A smooth, straightforward, frictionless experience — that is convenience.

Saw something interesting on Pinterest or Instagram? Do a screen shot, upload to Google search, and get the necessary information. Learn about it, ask other people, and buy it online from a recommended vendor. Receive the package the next day.

Need a passport photo? Pick up a smartphone or digital camera. Follow the basic rules of passport photos (Background, size, etc.), take a picture, edit it in a free passport software available online and everything is done at home, with ease. Again, convenient.

A Good Example — Starbucks

The company is a master in connecting bricks and clicks. The company connects the store, mobile app, and online experience.

Customers can order their drink, pick it up, scan their phone, and leave. They can order and stay. Or any other combination.

Customers earn points in the App for every buy. They can then send coupons and gifts to friends via the App too, turning them into brand advocates and favorites among their friends.

Speed up things — The speed of the service delivery has increased dramatically with technology. Customers expect fast, faster, fastest response from companies to their issues. How fast do they expect it? They go to the company's website, press the Chat button, and expect instantaneous help. They write a post on a Facebook wall and expect to get a quick response. They order things online and expect next day and even same day delivery.

An Interesting Fact

About 90% of customers consider an immediate response to their question to be within 10 minutes; 72% of customers expect a response to a complaint on social media in under an hour [1].

Paying by swiping the phone is faster than any other form of payment. Texting with the company is faster than emailing or calling. Sending a picture or a video to explain the issue at hand, instead of verbally explaining it, speeds-up understanding and accelerates the resolution of the issue. It also eliminates mistakes that may cause the need to repeat the service, slowing down things even more.

Boost proactivity — Technology helps companies move from passive service delivery (Waiting for customers to initiate the contact) to proactive service delivery (Contact customers first).

Technology can use big data analytics to interpret and understand customer behavioral patterns and use those insights to anticipate the customer's next move or need and proactively offer them information, appropriate suggestions, or important recommendations. For example, the company knows that many customers forget to write down the date for the next appointment. So the company sends them a WhatsApp reminder and also put it in their Google schedule.

Technology can detect problems that are about to happen and address them before the customer is even aware of a problem. For example, sending customers a reminder that their medicine is about to run out and they have to refill it. A simple alarm to remind a customer to take their medicine. British Gas uses technology to monitor heating and cooling appliances to know when maintenance is needed a moment before the machine breaks down rather than a moment after it does and the customer calls. This helps customers avoid failure and the high cost and consequences of down time.

Technology has allowed companies to detect and analyze customer word choice and emotions. Through text, speech and facial analysis, advanced software can assess the customer's mood, sentiment, and intent and advocate accordingly what an agent should say or do next proactively to deliver a better service. For example, a frustrated customer will be greeted differently than a happy customer. A sad customer will get more encouragement at the start of the conversation.

Build partnerships — Companies have hundreds and thousands of daily interactions with customers in a variety of service channels. During the interactions promises are made, information is transferred, help is provided, and solutions are offered. Technology can help the company follow every single interaction and everything that was done, if there is anything left open, and whether customers are satisfied with the outcome.

Technology can send each customer a short survey after every encounter, to see if they received the result they were hoping for or not. It can follow each customer's post-encounter key behavior variables such as product usage, purchase patterns, and service inquiries. It can identify customer dissatisfaction and churn signals, flag them, and make sure a service provider contacts the specific customer to ensure the continuation of the partnership. Technology ensures the service provider has a complete picture of what happened and what can be done prior to the contact. This ensures a higher rate of success in rectifying the mishaps and frustration, ensuring that customers don't fall through the cracks.

Set up try-on — Technology enables customers to check out products and see if they fit, without physically coming to the store. This creates a unique situation that enhances the experience and helps customers make better choices.

Sephora offers a mobile app called Makeup Artist that allows customers to virtually try on their face the company's makeup products. The customer can actually see how the makeup looks on them rather than on a model. The App also provides step-by-step instructions and tips on how to apply makeup based on the user's facial features along with product recommendations.

Warby Parker uses a similar software and the same concept but just with eye-wear. The company's App asks for a headshot and shows how different glasses look at each customer's unique face.

Virtual try-ons can also happen in physical stores. The physical store merges with the digital platform and becomes what is called Phygital (physical and digital). One example is Bonobos. The company, through its Guide-shop, invites customers to come for a virtual try-on experience. They come in the store, have a drink, and take a complete picture of their body. The smart dressing room can then virtually put on them any piece of clothing they selected previously. They can also add different accessories as well as shoes. Customers can consult an in-house fashion adviser. Customers then leave the store with no bags. The store has no inventory. They get what they bought delivered to their home at their preferred time.

A Good Example — Canada Goose

Canada Goose offers a special try-on for its customers. The company's stores use technology to create a Cold Room. This is a fitting room that can set temperatures to especially cold temperatures (–27 degrees Fahrenheit.) Inside, customers can put the company's jackets to the test. It's an experience that some customers see as a novelty, a chance to experience arctic temperatures, while others use it as a functional prop to get a sense of exactly what they need to keep warm.

Try-on reduces uncertainty to a minimum and cuts down dramatically on the number of sent back items (Around 40% of customers returned a non-defective item), avoiding that entire inconvenient and cumbersome process. Almost half of customers say that visual assistance dissuades them from returning a product [2].

Personalize — No two customers are alike. Technology can embrace customer individuality by using the company's data to customize and tailor the interaction to each customer preferences and personality. About 51% of US customers stated that they would be loyal to brands that know them and interact with them accordingly [3].

In the past, companies depended on employees to remember important information about customers and use it to provide a customized experience. No matter how talented employees are, they can't remember every customer's history and profile. Technology can. It combs through the tremendous amount of data and does in-depth intelligent analytics in milliseconds. It then uses machine learning to customize the experience for every single customer at every interaction. Google does it with personal Ads, Spotify with song proposals, Netflix with movie suggestions, or Facebook with friend recommendations. Maximizing individualization value.

A Good Example — Stitch Fix

Stitch Fix personalizes online cloth and accessories for each customer's needs, unique body, and personal fashion. It does it by using a questionnaire, fashion consultant, and an algorithm. The questionnaire provides insights into wants, needs, likes, dislikes, and more. The fashion consultant can analyze the information and personalize the right combinations of colors and dressmaking patterns. The algorithm looks at the history of purchases and returns patterns to understand what fits the customer, what they choose to keep, as well as what they choose to return.

Around 52% of products sent are purchased. With time, that figure goes up to 80%. Also, 83% of customers make a return purchase [4].

Canon uses technology to remotely monitor and collect information on its customers' copier machines, monitoring paper and ink usage, failures, etc. The company uses the information to understand the unique copier usage of each customer. This enables the company to provide personalized insights and advice for more efficient and effective copier management, reducing customers' printing costs and copier's breakdown, while improving their satisfaction from the company.

Information is crucial to the company's success but also important for customers to keep private. Overstepping privacy and personal data rules and regulations often ends poorly. The goal is to strike that perfect balance of spot-on relevancy to customers without becoming intrusive at any point along the way.

Surprise and delight — Technology can watch, learn, and understand which actions resonate and ultimately positively surprise customers and which don't. Over time, it can build a framework that seizes those opportunities when they occur and ensures that the right actions that previously led to positive surprise are taken in those situations. Surprise is based on timing — do the right thing, at the right time, to the right customer. Technology can make sure service providers seize the moment and take the necessary actions consistently. This makes it an integral part of day-to-day work and continually delighting customers.

Technology and the Way Customers Act and Interact

The rapid evolvement of technology has changed the way customers think, communicate, and behave. Customers have been slowly transforming into digital for years. The Covid-19 pandemic has accelerated that transformation. Technology has made people more empowered than ever. They can interact with a company by physically entering it, or go online and never set foot in the company again.

The digital world has also fundamentally changed customer expectations. Customers want to be able to interact and transact with companies across platforms when and where it suits them best. Done on their own terms, at their own time and pace, and anywhere that is convenient for them. Clicks and voice-activated interactions are now preferred over telephone or face-to-face interactions. Coming physically to the company or waiting for someone to answer the phone are considered a burden and perceived as a waste of time. Companies have to adapt accordingly to avoid becoming obsolete.

The digitally-oriented customer has several characteristics (Figure 7.5):

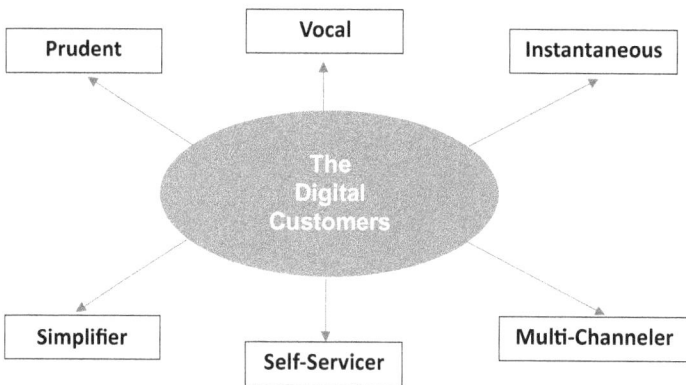

Figure 7.5. The Digitally-oriented Customer Facets

Prudent — Customers use technology to do research. By looking through online rating sites, forums, and social media they learn about the characteristics of the company's products and services, customer reviews, prices, and customer satisfaction scores; they can even read the company's social responsibility manifesto. They talk to other customers to learn from their experience. After accumulating all the information, they can smartly decide whether the company is worth their hard-earned money.

Companies can't hide information and problems anymore. Customers will find the truth. Being transparent and sharing information is key to winning customers over. Otherwise, customers will quickly switch, with one click, to another competitor they heard does things better.

Vocal — Customers are more vocal than ever before. They share, post, and upload videos, stories, and remarks regarding their experiences. Social media and other web-based platforms provide a gigantic megaphone in which customers can voice their opinions for thousands to hear. It has never been this easy and so influential to be heard — for better or for worse. Customers know that posting a few words on the web gains companies attention and gets them to handle their situation.

Companies can use vocal customers to their favor. Amplifying the voices of satisfied and loyal customers. Encouraging them to express their authentic experience by talking about it, sharing valuable information, or leaving a positive comment on the company's website.

Instantaneous — Customers live in an instant gratification world. They hold a smartphone in their hand that allows them to get food, tickets to a show, transportation or a movie, in only a few clicks. They can answer messages and emails immediately throughout the day. Customers expect companies to also be connected, like offering immediate response from purchase to complaint resolution. Customers who go to a website and can't find what they want in a few seconds bounce back to the search engine and move to the next options.

In a hyper-connected world, companies can't afford to be slow. They have to switch to the fast lane where customers are already in.

Simplifiers — Customers expect interaction with companies to be hassle-free, with uncomplicated requirements and no lengthy processes. They want valuable, relevant, and precise information that will help them achieve their desired goal. No hard work, back and forth correspondence, or any other annoying nuances.

Companies have to go through the customer journey and see where it's unfriendly or uncooperative and fix those hurdles. This simply prevents problems and failures.

Self-servicers — Customers are tech-savvy and expect companies to provide start-to-finish effective self-service options for any issue. This gives them the flexibility to do what they need on their own terms.

Companies that build the right self-service infrastructure help customers serve themselves, creating a win-win situation. Customers get the channel they prefer, and the company reduces costs dramatically.

Multi-channelers — Customers, in their day-to-day lives, communicate through a variety of channels. They also expect companies to provide service through multiple channels, allowing them the flexibility to choose the channel that best fits their specific situation.

Companies have to ensure the level of experience is the same across all channels. They must provide an integrated and seamless experience even when the interaction starts at one channel (for example, phone) and end at another (social media).

The digital customer "consults" their smartphones first. If an App or algorithm can deliver what they need, the better. If nothing else works, they will talk to a human, but thinking it could have been done differently. They hate being contacted for unnecessary or mundane stuff like information they already gave several times in the past. They expect automated, instant confirmation for everything done with the company. They get peeved when they can't find elementary information on the website. The digital customer wants to be in the driver seat controlling the encounter. The company intervenes only when things break down or customers ask for help. This is what customers crave and they appreciate it when it happens.

Conclusion

Technology is a disruptor mechanism. It's rewriting and reshaping the rules for how service and experiences are delivered and how companies should be managed. It's making the old way of customer service inefficient and often irrelevant. Social, mobile, and software platforms are technology tools that accelerate the opportunity for companies to truly expand the relationships and engagement with customers.

Technology isn't a passing trend. Its influence on service delivery will only rise in the foreseeable future. Companies should embrace technology to optimize both their internal and external services, and fulfill the digital customer's expectations. Getting technology wrong or just doing the bare minimum will result in an eroding level of experiences and dissatisfied customers.

References

[1] Hunersen, C. (2019). Why Amazon is a Leader in Customer Experience. XM Blog. Available at https://www.qualtrics.com/blog/amazon-customer-experience-leader/

[2] Mort, A. (2019). 2019 Consumer Electronics Survey: NFF Returns. TechSee. Available at https://techsee.me/blog/nff-survey/#:~:text=2019%20Survey%3A%20NFF%20Returns&text=The%20survey%20demonstrates%20that%2041,and%2Dmortar%20and%20online%20retailers

[3] Shaham, H. (2018). 4 Technology Based Solutions to Successful Customer Retention Strategies. Available at https://techsee.me/blog/technology-based-solutions-to-enhance-customer-retention-strategies/

[4] Goodwater Thesis, (2017). Understanding Stitch Fix: Finding the Perfect Fit. Available at https://www.goodwatercap.com/thesis/understanding-stitch-fix

Lecture 8

Service Managerial Leadership

"Organizations exist to serve. Period. Leaders live to serve. Period."

Tom Peters

What is the best management style for maximizing employee performance? Getting them to deliver great customer experiences?

Over the years, academics and practitioners have written hundreds of books about management and leadership. Peter Drucker, Ken Blanchard, Daniel Goleman, Bernard Bass, Linda Hill, and many others have presented a broad range of methods, models, approaches, and theories. The world's successful leaders have been profiled to find what key characteristics contribute to their success. The abundance of studies has provided no clear winner for the best managerial style. Yet one truth is consistently reiterated: Managers have the biggest influence on employee satisfaction, motivation, and success at work. This is why people come to organizations but leave managers.

Employees invest in their work as much as their manager invests in them — no more, no less. The way they treat customers mirrors the way managers treat them. Consequently, employee behaviors, actions, and attitudes reflect their manager's behavior, actions, and attitude. This phenomenon isn't unique to manager-employee relationships. Interactions at all levels of the hierarchy have the same dynamics. It's called the "chain of influence" and it happens in every organization.

The chain of influence is a powerful phenomenon that starts at the top with the CEO. From there, it ripples through one managerial level to the next. The way the CEOs behave toward their vice presidents determines how the vice presidents treat the managers who report to them. This influence continues down the managerial hierarchy, eventually determining how front-line managers treat their employees.

The chain of influence can also jump ranks. The way a CEO or a vice president treats a front-line manager affects their behavior toward his or her employees. The chain of influence does not stop with employees. Not surprisingly, the way employees are treated by their manager determines their behavior toward customers.

The chain of influence results in either a positive or negative outcome; it's never neutral. A *positive* outcome leads to positive relationships between individuals (both managers and employees), a better internal and external service experience, and improved business results. A *negative* outcome leads to opposite results: Poor relationships, underperformance, and mediocrity. Understanding the actions that lead to a positive chain is the key to being a successful manager.

When Bosses 'serve' their employees, everything improves (see Figure 8.1 on the next page).

The Source of Poor Performance

Managers often rush to blame employees for underperformance or providing poor customer service. But are employees really at fault? Often, the answer is "No." In fact, employees do the work and deliver the service, but the manager is the one who determines employees' level of performance. This shouldn't come as a surprise. Given the chain of influence, before blaming the employee,

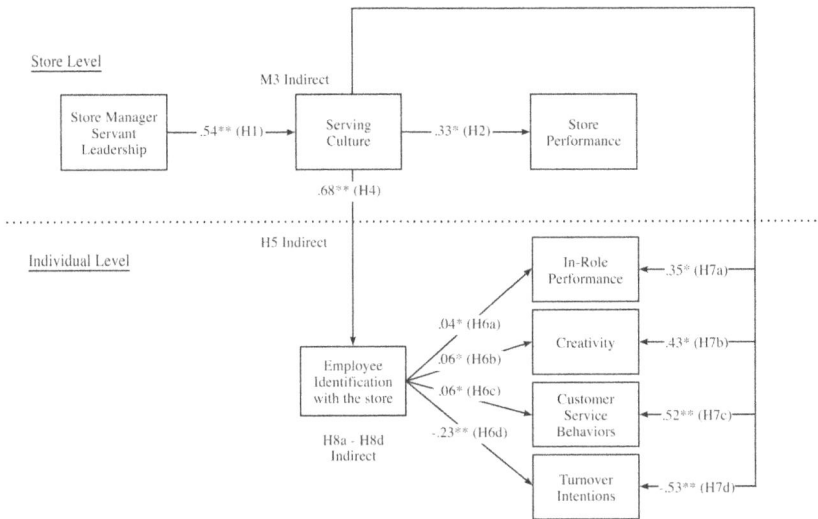

Figure 8.1. Managers' Influence on Employees' Service Performance

Source: R. C. Liden, S. J. Wayne, C. Liao, J. D. Meuser. **Servant Leadership and Serving Culture: Influence on Individual and Unit Performance.** *Academy of Management Journal*, 2013; 57 (5): 1434 DOI: 10.5465/amj.2013.0034

managers have to first look in the mirror and analyze their own actions and behaviors. Did they cause employees to underperform? If employees ignore customer requests and show apathy toward customers' problems, a manager's first response should be to ask, "Do I ignore my employees' requests? Do I show apathy when I talk to them?". If employees don't keep their promises, managers should ask whether they keep all the promises they make to employees.

Managers' self-analysis is an integral part of achieving success. They have to see themselves as others see them and keep an open mind while listening to criticism and comments from people around them. This is the best way to understand if they themselves are doing something unsound instead of blaming employees for problems.

Finding out which of their behaviors might result in negative consequences is the first step. Then they need to make changes in their behavior. Analyzing and changing their own behaviors prompts employees to follow suit. In turn, they will analyze the effectiveness of their own actions before blaming the customers for every problem. Changing behavior and eliminating the "blame game" creates a cycle of success. It boosts employee morale, increases employee and customer satisfaction, and improves overall performance.

Successful Managers are Service Providers

In his book *Leading for Growth*, Ray Davis, the highly successful CEO of Umpqua Bank, wrote the following:

> I am the company's president and CEO only when I participate in formal events. That's when I represent the company, or when I'm on the phone talking about quarterly results with Wall Street analysts. The rest of the time, I'm neither president nor CEO. Everyone in the bank knows it, and my business card shows it, too. I am "Head of Support." Our work changes on a daily basis. There are problems, issues, and needs for improvement. This is my job. The bank's management team and I are here to serve the people in the organization: to prevent errors, remove barriers, and provide people with everything they need to carry out their jobs to the best of their ability [1].

Managers at any level, in any company, in every industry worldwide are in the same business: The "People business." Managing employees, developing customer relations, dealing with suppliers, and interacting daily with colleagues. All of which revolve around people. Being successful in the people business depends primarily on a manager's ability to develop a positive, long-lasting relationship with others — especially with employees. A great manager-employee relationship leads to cooperation and mutual understanding and a positive working environment. This motivates employees to cooperate and build long-lasting relationships with customers (see Figure 8.2 on the next page).

Building strong relationships with employees isn't easy for managers who follow common managerial practices. To be successful,

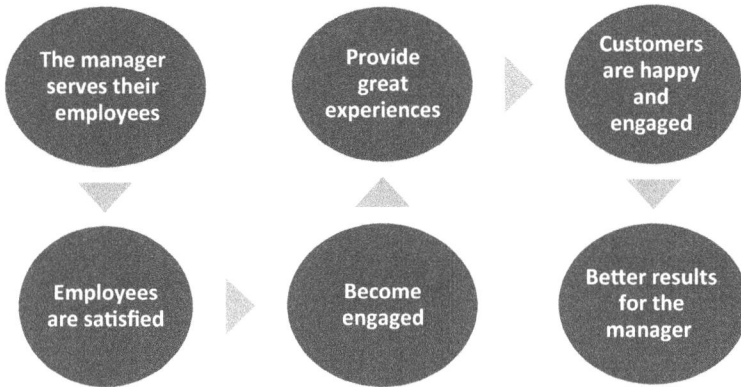

Figure 8.2. The Manager Service-Oriented Influence Chain

managers must follow Ray Davis' path — provide excellent service to employees and support them. With that in mind, managers have to view employees as allies and partners, not as tools or a means to an end. They have to motivate employees by lighting a fire within them rather than coercing them to do their jobs by lighting a fire underneath them. Consequently, the managers' level of success comes down to their willingness to place their employees' needs before their own.

Placing employees' needs first and providing service aren't acts of novelty or kindness. They are logical, results-driven activities. Employees mirror their manager. By taking care of employees and giving them more, managers get more in return. They gain an engaged group of people who do a great job and take care of customers. This is a win-win situation. When both sides win, higher goals and superior results are easier to achieve. By thinking of employees' needs first, the manager creates a *positive* chain of influence, maximizes employees' potential, and as a result, achieves success [2].

Take an underperforming team, department, or even an organization and replace the manager in charge with someone who uses a managerial way that is characterized by being a service provider and placing employees first. The same employees, conditions, limitations, and pay exist, but now they are led by a manager who develops a personal relationship with them, helps fulfill their needs, resolves their problems, and provides unexpected positive surprises. After a few months, reexamine the team's, department's, or organization's performance. You will find happier employees who are engaged in their work and a dramatic improvement in every aspect of performance and results. Customers will suddenly receive a more personal, caring experience that is tailored to their needs.

The Three Elements of Service-Oriented Managerial Leadership

When the manager delivers to employees a wonderful working experience every day, they, in turn, mirror those effort toward customers. It's reflection management. To deliver experiences to employees, managers have to adopt a service-oriented managerial leadership style. It is based on three elements: Listening, delivering, surprising (Figure 8.3).

1. **Listening** — The manager gathers information and learns everything about employees. Then, they build a profile for each

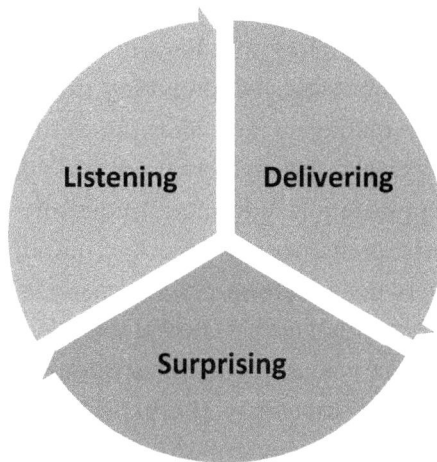

Figure 8.3. The Elements of Successful Service Oriented Leadership

employee and understand what they need, what limitations they have, and what challenges they face.

2. **Delivering** — The manager provides excellent service to employees, satisfying their needs, building strong rapport, and helping them succeed.

3. **Surprising** — The manager does things beyond what's expected. Going the extra mile and providing employees with something special and exciting that makes them say "Wow" and become engaged at work.

These three elements aren't random. Rather, they resemble a successful service encounter: Listen to the customers and understand their needs, deliver a service experience that fulfills those needs, and go beyond the scope of the request to make customers say "Wow" and become loyal and engaged. Given that managers are service providers, any interaction with employees is, in fact, a service encounter and a teaching moment. When the manager executes the three elements in their daily thinking, conduct, and actions continuously, the standard for employees to follow is set. By making these actions a habit, the manager provides a personal example for a successful encounter that reflects in employee actions when they do the work and interact with internal as well as external customers.

Two Questions Every Manager Should Ask

Many companies are making customer experience a strategic priority. Improving customer experience is difficult to get right, because the primary hurdle is translating boardroom vision for a superior customer experience into action at the front line. This is why managers are so important. It's their job to make it happen. Two questions should guide managers in making experiences a reality:

1. Do I place my employees before work?
2. Do I love my work and my employees?

Question 1: Do I place employees before work?

A manager who places employees before work is assigning a priority to their needs, state of mind, and satisfaction. The focus is on their wellbeing and perceiving them as human beings rather than robots or a means to an end.

In choosing this path, managers develop their employees, constantly invest in them, and make them feel important. Placing employees first gets them on board. It makes them feel important and that someone cares about them. Creating a family-like working place that puts a smile on employees' faces and motivates them to do great work. Doing whatever it takes to help their manager and the company succeed. Placing customers first and working towards making them happy.

Placing work before employees, on the other hand, assigns a higher priority to productivity and operations than to what employees need. Efficiency becomes the key word and improving productivity the main goal. In that environment, employees are asked to work faster, increase their productivity, and avoid wasting time. The manager focuses on meeting deadlines, achieving sales targets, and making sure every employee adheres to the efficiency metrics. Employees become tools to reach organizational goals and are treated accordingly. Putting work before employees leads to employees who punch the clock, become disengaged and indifferent, and deliver average performance at best. These employees often put their work before customers and at times even ignore them. People's emotions become irrelevant. In fact, managers can become so obsessed with goals and standards, they often forget that first and foremost, they manage people.

Placing employees before work isn't about being nice, kind, or generous. Rather, it's the best path to turn the average employee into an engaged one, an average department to a successful one and a mediocre organization to a leading one.

An Interesting Fact

There is a tremendous gap in performance on employee engagement between those companies in top quartile and those at the bottom quartile.

Top quartile companies achieved:

18% higher productivity
10% higher customer loyalty
30% lower turnover
81% lower absenteeism
23% higher profitability [3].

Engaged employees are an asset that significantly influence the company's success. It's no coincidence that the best companies in the world put their people first and have a significantly larger percentage of engaged employees than companies that don't. Thus, enjoying a higher performance and consistently maintaining a competitive advantage over time.

Question 2: Do I love my work and my employees?

Love is a word people tend to avoid in the business world. Some say mixing love with money, work, or profit degrades the word. Nevertheless, when love is linked to management practices, it means being human and sensitive, considering others' needs, and building sincere, long-term personal relationships with others.

Ask people about a great manager they work for, and a common response will probably be, "We love our manager. We will do anything for our manager." Employees who love their manager trust, follow, and do what they ask. They are inspired to do their best and go the extra mile. Such a relationship positively influences their state of mind and fosters a positive working environment.

Southwest Airlines flies more than 100 million passengers every year. It's consistently mentioned as one of the best places to work, and it excels in customer service. In an industry where bankruptcy is common, Southwest has been profitable for four decades. When Herb Kelleher, the founder of Southwest Airlines was asked about the secret of his company's success, he simply answered "Love." He pointed at a flight crew who had just come off an airplane and the ground crew that arrived to do maintenance as he talked about how they love what they do, their customers, and each other. He added, "They love their managers, and they even love me. And they are loved back." Their managers treat them well and help them be successful at work. As a result, Southwest people wake up every morning happy to come to work and motivated to serve customers [4].

The company doesn't keep "love" a secret. It's openly expressed through the company's heart-shaped logo and its stock symbol LUV. Over the years, Kelleher has claimed "love" is the company's biggest competitive advantage because competitors can't copy it. He added that "love" is the underlying theme that enabled the company to achieve tremendous results and beat its competitors in almost every area: Productivity, quality of service, efficiency in operations, and business results.

Why do employees come to work? Is it because they love what they do and have fun while working? Or is it to collect a paycheck? Those who come only for the paycheck will get the job done. But if they love what they do, they will give the company and its customers their blood, sweat, and tears. There is a reason the most successful people fall into one of two categories: They love what they do, or they do what they love.

To succeed, managers must love their employees, love being with them, working with them, investing in them, and helping them. The love must be evident to employees when they reach new highs and even more when they experience new lows. It's difficult to love employees when they disappoint and fail, but these are times when love and support count the most. That's exactly what employees need to get through tough times. In the end, the love that managers shower on employees will positively reflect in their positive attitudes toward those managers, their jobs, and customers they serve.

Of course, saying, "I love my employees, and I love what I do" are just words. Employees expect to see daily actions that turn these words into reality. Love is built gradually over time through actions.

Personalizing Management

Every employee is different, with different wants, needs, and thought processes. Managing all employees uniformly is ineffective; the manager's specific management style will suit some but not others. As a result, only a few will be satisfied, and success will be capped. Expecting employees to adjust themselves to the manager's managerial style is futile. To break through and maximize employees' potential, managers have to personalize their management style, customizing it to fit each employee's profile — personality, needs, and outlook. That means doing something to cause one employee to say "Wow" and feel special, while doing the same thing to a different employee causes him or her to say "OK" and show indifference. The better the fit between the managerial action and the employee's profile, both the manager and employees win.

Advancements in artificial intelligence (AI) can help enhance personalization. AI can find correlations between employees' interactions with the manager and performance. Taking this data with each employee profile, the AI can provide managers with relevant information such as "To get this employee to perform better, here are the information/skills/abilities you should give or teach them." Strengthening each employee, the right way. Maximizing results.

A good example is giving a bonus to employees for doing excellent work. Let's say the standard bonus is a dinner for two in a gourmet restaurant. If the employee is a food fan and likes fine dining, this bonus makes him happy, and he will say "Wow!" But if the employee has a newborn at home and dining out is a hassle, the bonus' appeal will be muted and its effect marginal at best. But what if this employee is a big fan of a certain basketball team? The right bonus for him is two tickets with excellent seats to that team's next game, provided the cost is comparable to a dinner for two. When he gets this bonus, this basketball fan who has talked about this game a lot would say "Wow!" Personalizing the bonus makes both employees happy and excited. Their connection to the manager becomes stronger and motivation rides high. There is no doubt giving individualized bonuses is harder than generic ones. But it's worth the effort because it turns an average employee into an engaged one.

Personalized management isn't only about bonuses and compensation. It can be applied to other facets of an employee's work. For example, when an employee raises a substantial work-related issue, the manager who knows this person's abilities and preferences can seize this opportunity to do something beyond what's expected. The manager might say to that employee, "You are in charge; you find a way to fix the problem. I support your decision." The employee who likes to take the initiative will be positively surprised and feel great knowing the manager trusts him or her. This action gives the employee something special he wants and doesn't receive every day. As a result, he will work hard to prove himself and therefore put more time and extra effort into finding the solution. After the problem is fixed, the feeling of accomplishment and the drive to look for more problems to fix will continue. This is a positive spiral that results from a win-win situation.

Similar action can be taken when it comes to new ideas and suggestions. When the right employee with the appropriate abilities makes the right suggestion, the manager can say, "Take this idea and make it happen!" In this case, the employee should be asked to prepare a strategic plan for implementing the idea and, once he is ready, they can meet to make it a reality. Positively surprising the employee and giving them the opportunity to make the needed change and implement the necessary improvement. For the employee, work becomes more interesting. It pushes them to keep looking for ideas to improve. For the manager, valuable time is saved and the system itself constantly improves; again, a win-win situation.

An Interesting Fact

About 70% of American employees are disengaged, costing the US over $550 billion a year in lost productivity [5].

Companies that invest in personalization to individual needs and creating an employee experience are four times more profitable than those that don't [6].

Personalized management is about knowing how to challenge each employee to improve the quality of work they do. It's also about assigning tasks that tap employees' strengths rather than involve their weaknesses. Putting employees in a position where they can succeed rather than struggle or even fail. When employees are in the right place, assigned the right tasks, and are challenged effectively, they show devotion and excel.

At first, personalization requires extra effort, time, and investment from a manager. But this investment is worth it. The positive effect that personalized management has on employees is tremendous. Employees enjoy work and personalize interactions with every customer they meet. As time goes by, personalization happens naturally and seamlessly and thus becomes simpler to execute. When both managers and employees personalize the way they operate, great experiences become a habit.

Conclusion

Managers look for new technologies, new marketing tools, and new operational ways to achieve a competitive advantage and improve profitability. Unfortunately, they often overlook the most important component to profitability and success — their managerial skills.

Employees do the work, produce products, and deliver experiences. But it's the manager who determines the level of performance. Subsequently, a manager who wants to achieve exceptional results has to be exceptional in the way they manage people.

Managers in companies that provide exceptional service supervise people differently. No matter how high their position is in the hierarchy, they serve employees. When managers are service providers, a positive success spiral is created. Employees are inspired to do excellent work. They are happy, excited about coming to work every day, and deliver exceptional experiences to customers. Employees' positive actions lead customers to spend more money and provide positive word-of-mouth. Customers' actions, in turn, help managers achieve higher-level goals and better business results. Yes, happy employees lead to happy customers, which leads to happy managers. It's that simple.

References

[1] Davis, R. (2007). Leading for Growth. Jossey-Bass. San-Francisco, CA, p. 61.
[2] Hsieh, T. (2010). Delivering Happiness. Business Plus. NewYork, NY.
[3] Gallup, (2016). What is Employee Engagement and How Do You Improve It? Available at https://www.gallup.com/workplace/285674/improve-employee-engagement-workplace.aspx
[4] Johnson, M.E., and Hall, J.M. (2009). Enhancing Service at Southwest Airlines. Vincent L. Lacorte Case Studies, Tuck School of Business at Dartmouth.
[5] Duncan, J. (2018). How to Refine Your Management Style and Boost Employee Engagement. Available at https://blog.bonus.ly/how-to-refine-your-management-style-and-boost-employee-engagement
[6] Lahey, S. (2019). The Future Employee Experience is Personalized. Availableathttps://www.zendesk.com/blog/future-employee-experience-personalized/

Lecture 9

A Customer-Focused
Human Resources (HR)

"Traditional corporations are organized for efficiency. Or consistency. But not JOY. Joy comes from surprise and connection and humanity and transparency and new...If you fear special requests, if you staff with cogs, if you have to put it all in a manual, then the chances of amazing someone are really quite low."

Seth Godin

How important are employees in organizations? Not in words, but in actions — investment of money and resources?

Employees on stage and backstage take care of customers' issues and determine the level of experience delivered and satisfaction achieved. This cause companies to state: "Employees are our greatest asset", "Employees are the face of the company", and "Excellent employees are a competitive advantage." However, a gap exists between what is said about the importance of employees and what is done.

Employees are touted as the face of the company, but they are the first to go when a crisis occurs and revenue goes south. Employees are proclaimed as crucial to the success of the company, but often receive only a touch above minimum wage and basic benefits. Customer-oriented human resources has to narrow and eventually eliminate these gaps if the goal is great experiences.

Companies go as far as employees take them. Happy employees perform on the highest level and lead the company to success. Disgruntled employees lead to dissatisfied customers and mediocre performance. Even one unhappy employee can create substantial problems by negatively influencing customers.

A simple, well-defined equation exists in any organization. Service providers determine customer experience. Human Resources (HR) influences the service providers and their level of engagement and motivation to serve. If service providers' level of engagement determine the quality of the customer experience and HR influences the service providers' level of engagement, then HR plays a critical role in determining the level of customer experience. Thus, it influences the company's financial performance (Figure 9.1).

High employee engagement is a must when it comes to delivering experience.

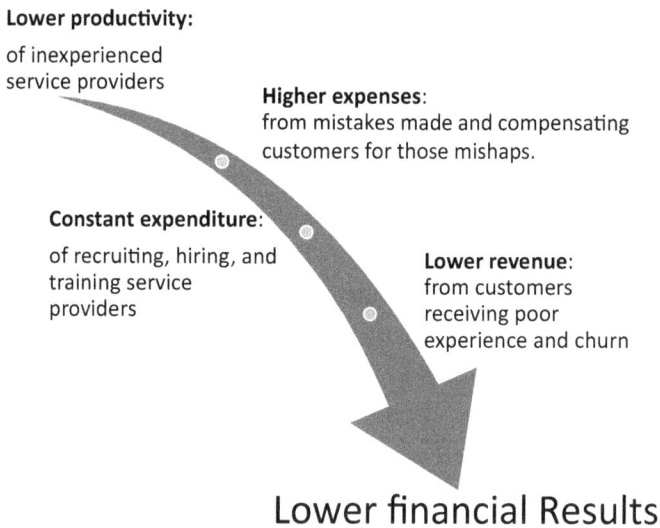

Lower productivity:
of inexperienced service providers

Higher expenses:
from mistakes made and compensating customers for those mishaps.

Constant expenditure:
of recruiting, hiring, and training service providers

Lower revenue:
from customers receiving poor experience and churn

Lower financial Results

Figure 9.1. The Costs of a Non-Customer-Focused HR

An Interesting Fact

Companies with engaged employees outperform by 10% in customer ratings, 21% in productivity, and 22% in profitability.

Furthermore, they show significantly lower absenteeism (−37%), turnover (−25% to −68%), and safety incidents (−48%) [1].

An effective customer-oriented HR operates on three levels:

- **The individual level** — Understand how to enhance service providers' performance and motivate them to deliver great experiences.
- **The team level** — Understand how to improve group work and cross-department collaboration to improve the internal customer service.
- **The organizational level** — Understand how to improve the working environment and change with the business environment to uncover new opportunities to mitigate service risk and maintain success.

This lecture focuses on what it means to make HR customer-oriented. It starts with incorporating the right customer-focused building blocks and customer-focused goals.

Building Blocks for Customer-focused HR

HR building blocks set guidelines and standards for every decision and action taken by the company toward its employees. When these building blocks are service-oriented, it's easier for people to deliver great experiences. Here are several of those building blocks that should be in every company (see Figure 9.2 on the next page).

Employees are the #1 asset — Given that service providers determine whether customers come back or not, they are a very important asset to the company and not a cost. Just like any other asset,

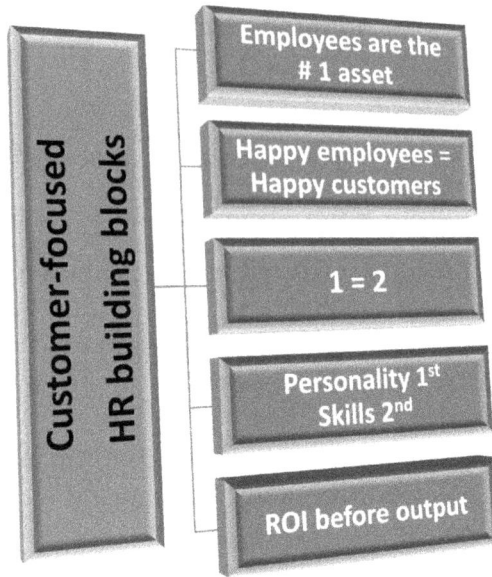

Figure 9.2. Customer-Oriented HR Building Blocks

they should be developed and enhanced. Unlike any other asset however, employees are assets that leave the organization every day. HR has to make sure they come back day after day, ready to serve customers.

Happy employees = Happy customers — Employees serve customers and they are the face of the company. Happy employees with smiling faces more often than not, lead to happy customers with smiling faces and vice versa when employees are unhappy and frustrated. HR has to make sure employees are happy and inspired.

1 = 2 — The equation isn't a misprint. It means that one exceptional employee equals two average employees in terms of performance and the quality of service provided. Talent is the ball game. Exceptional employees don't just deliver great experiences, they also elevate everyone's achievements around them. Keeping those employees satisfied and loyal is crucial to the success of the company.

Personality 1st, skills 2nd — Personality determines the individual pattern of thinking, emotions, and behavior. Given that personality can't be taught or changed, it comes first. Knowledge and skills can be taught and changed and thus come second. A service encounter is a personal encounter. The personality of employees plays a critical role in their ability to deal effectively with customers. Personality is also important in the cultural fit to the company and interaction with other people. A personality fit can be the difference between a successful and productive working environment and one where employees are unhappy or hostile toward each other.

ROI before outputs — HR budget is often perceived as a cost that can be trimmed. To change that perception, HR has to embrace terms such as ROI (Return on Investment) instead of outputs and expenses. Showing everyone in the company that the budget it receives yields positive outcomes (customer satisfaction and loyalty) that increases income (customer spending) and reduces costs (less turnover, mistakes, and repeat service). Thus, demonstrating its meaningful contribution to the company's financial performance.

Goals for Customer-focused HR

HR has a unique place in the company. It's the entrance gate for every candidate who looked for a position and every employee who was hired. It's also the exit gate in which every employee who leaves the company goes through. In between, HR deals with and provides service to every department and every person in the organization. It's the address that people with personal questions, problems, requests, and issues go to.

By commending such an important position, it has major influence on people's experiences and perceptions. By listening, observing, advising, and providing a concierge-like internal service, it sets an example for excellent service that everyone can follow. It helps the company in its quest to get everyone focused on customers and deliver exceptional experiences. By being customer-centric, HR can better understand every department's needs and find ways to make every interaction effortless, making internal customers happy. To do that, HR has several goals to achieve.

Implement the customer-first strategy and culture — Delivering a winning customer experience requires a joined up agenda across the business. Given that HR interacts with everyone in the organization, its goal is to implement the customer-first agenda. HR has to adopt the objectives of the service-first strategy as well as the customer-obsessed values and follow them in every decision and action. From selecting new people to removing barriers that hinder performance all the way to making sure service achievement are loudly celebrated. Every person interacting with HR should see what a great experience looks like, ingraining the customer-centric message publicly.

Reduce turnover — High employee turnover equals poor experience. High turnover means a large number of new employees with limited knowledge and skills are serving customers. They struggle to perform their job diligently. The combination of limited professionalism and longer handling time frustrates customers. It places more burden on existing employees who become frustrated for having to do more work at usually the same compensation.

Consistent high turnover creates a negative culture where uncertainty is high and the ability to build friendly relationships among employees and with customers is low. Such a culture has the most negative influence on the best employees. Talented employees have options, and a negative environment sends them away.

Personalize the interaction — HR should use the wealth of information that the company has on each employee to personalize the interaction and treat them individually the way they want to be treated. Employees who receive personalized interaction within the company will often mirror those actions and personalize the interaction when they interact with customers.

Upgrade employees' capabilities — Many employees are worried about being replaced by technology while others are uncertain if their current skillset will be enough in the future. Those fears aren't entirely misplaced. New technology is going to have a big impact on the workplace as we currently know it, changing both workflow and types of employment.

HR has to make sure the importance of people in delivering experience isn't forgotten by preparing them for the future workplace, helping them upgrade their technical skills as well as interpersonal skills that computers can't replace.

Manage service knowledge — Knowledge sharing across the company is critical to delivering exceptional experiences. HR has to inspire people to document failures and success in serving customers. Then, find knowledge sharing strategies to distribute the information. Allowing employees to duplicate successful actions, avoid failure, and thus improve the level of customer experience. This saves time and energy, improves productivity, reduces unnecessary costs, and delivers a more consistent level of service.

Another aspect of knowledge management is making sure people's comprehensive knowledge stays within the company's walls if they leave. When an experienced individual leaves, the business doesn't just lose him or her, it also loses the knowledge they acquired throughout their tenure. That knowledge is valuable, and HR has to make sure it's documented in the company's information systems.

Create a great place to work — Customer experience is often a reflection of employee experience at the workplace. HR should promote a fun, healthy, and prosperous work environment that employees enjoy being part of. HR has to listen to employees and provide perks and small gestures that make the workplace more enjoyable, making it easier to attract and retain top talent.

Prepare for future service trends — As time passes, the business environment and customer needs and wants change. HR has to be aware of those changes and even anticipate trends that will influence service providers in the future. Then, plan how to make the necessary changes to deal with those developments. Make sure great experiences are continually delivered.

When all the goals above are achieved, employees are all-in on delivering experiences to customers. They become more team and solution-oriented, show a positive attitude and passion for learning, and go above what is expected.

Reaching the goals discussed above helps HR set the foundation needed to deliver exceptional experiences. The next step is building customer-oriented HR practices.

Customer-Oriented HR Practices

Human role in serving customers is changing. Artificial Intelligent Bots and self-service technology are taking over the simple and mundane service interaction that employees used to do. That leaves employees with the tasks that technology still can't do — dealing with complicated issues and unique challenges that require in-depth thinking and creativity. Building relationships with customers and being there for people who need to talk to a human when things go terribly wrong is one such task. Performing these tasks require smart and proficient service providers. HR has to make sure this is the case.

HR can use its different practices to make sure everyone in the company is service-centered and customer-oriented. Specifically, there are three practices that are going to be outlined in detail in the following pages (see Figure 9.3 on the next page).

Selecting service-oriented people

Employee selection is HR's most important practice. The stakes are high for choosing the right person for service jobs. A mistake can't be fixed by training or compensation and it can lead to dramatic negative ramifications. Approximately 80% of customers won't

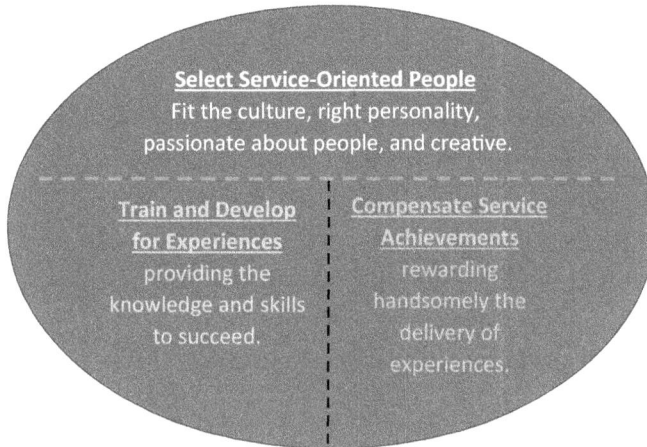

Figure 9.3. Customer-Oriented HR Practices

return to a company after a bad customer experience with an employee. Also, the wrong fit leads to that person either quitting or being dismissed. The cost of replacing an employee is about 20% of annual salary for mid-level positions. Between lost revenue from customers, selection costs, and onboarding of a new employee, every wrong decision becomes a drain on HR resources and the company's bottom line [2]. This is why selection decisions shouldn't be rushed and resources should be invested in creating an effective selection system that yields service-oriented people.

While there isn't a full-proof system to select the right person, there are three key steps that can increase the chances of getting it right:

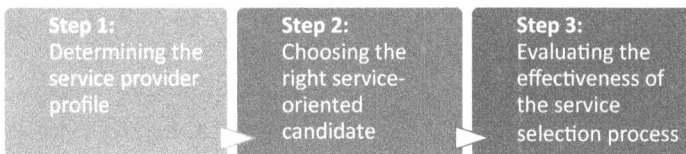

Step 1: Determining the service provider profile

Selecting the right person starts with understanding the desired profile and attributes needed to fill the service position. The job description should articulate the necessary knowledge and skillset. Equally important is articulating the right personality and values that fit well into the customer-centric culture. When building the profile and job description, it's a good idea to think about the skills the person must bring into the job from day one, and what skills can be learned through training later on, without jeopardizing the quality of service.

The service-oriented job description is the interface between the company's hiring service standards and the outside world candidates, setting a level by which every candidate is compared and chosen, with no compromise. An effective job description helps attract qualified applicants and sets the service vibe for those going to be hired. Reducing the number of inadequate candidates, saving time and effort in the hiring process.

Step 2: Choosing the right service-oriented candidate

Choosing the right employee is a challenge. The company is trying to uncover the personality and skillset of each candidate to understand if he or she fits the company's culture and the service position. The candidate, on the other hand, attempts to present an array of qualification while covering any flaws, to portray a person the company will want to hire. It's a "game" that the company has to master if it wants to select employees that can deliver experiences.

In choosing a candidate, fit with the company comes before the most skilled. The right fit means the candidate is compatible with the company's vision, culture, and values. The candidates believe in what the company believes in, and are passionate about helping people. The most skilled means the candidate has the talent to deliver upon the company's standards. Fit comes first because highly talented employees might produce good results in the short-term, but the culture-misfit often causes more harm than good over the long haul.

There are additional benefit in choosing fit before most skilled. First, technical skills can be taught while it's next to impossible to teach someone to be friendly, enthusiastic that genuinely cares about people, or build interpersonal relationships with them. Second, employees without experience can be molded according to the company's vision and values. They didn't acquire bad habits that have to be changed. They don't show service fatigue and are open to trying different ways of doing things.

In choosing the right candidate there is no compromising. Every candidate has to pass the standards, no exceptions. The goal isn't to choose the best candidate out of a pool of candidates. If none of the candidates in the pool meet the standards, nobody is selected, and another group of candidates is assembled. Compromising the selection standards hurts the company in several ways. First, the candidate won't be able to deliver the necessary experiences. Second, existing employees see that the standards are compromised and quickly fall in-line with the reduced level of service performance. Finally, customers who are used to a certain level of service will experience a lower level which will negatively influence them.

Great experience requires great people. Hiring the right people makes the onboarding simpler and faster. People in the company accept them and have no problem working with them. When people like the people around them, they communicate and cooperate better, which leads to a better working environment, and everyone performs on a higher level.

Tools for selecting service-oriented people

Getting service-oriented people requires specific tools aimed at understanding if the candidate has what is needed to effectively interact with customers and deliver great experiences. Here are five major tools:

A customer service aptitude test — A scientifically validated psychometric tool designed to analyze the most important traits of personality that influence one's customer service aptitude and is instrumental in determining how individuals perform in service jobs [3].

Role play interview — A scenario-based interaction between the candidate and the interviewer. The candidate is put in a position to truly test his or her customer service orientation — empathy, positivity, and patience. It allows the interviewer to see how the candidate handles uncomfortable situations (an angry or frustrated customer) and behave under pressure (Dealing with several issues at once). This is the closest way to see an authentic preview of what a customer will get if the candidate is selected.

Service exam — The candidate gets two or three open ended questions that represent service challenges they might encounter in their future job. The answers to the question provide a good glimpse of the candidate's frame-of-mind. The length, depth, and detail of the answers provide a good sense of the candidate's enjoyment of delivering service.

Reality check — Taking candidates at hectic hours to the place where they are going to work. Showing them live what they are getting into. Seeing is better than hearing. It gives candidates an accurate picture of what to expect. It's also a good way to see how they react to situations — positive or negative — an important tell in choosing the right candidate.

Employees' perspective — Candidates who come to an interview meet the receptionist, the security guards, the office manager, and others. All those people should be asked to pay attention and evaluate the level of friendliness and politeness that these candidates express. When candidates don't think anyone is watching, they act naturally and show their true selves. If at those moments they show service-oriented traits, that is an excellent sign of a good fit. Also, candidates should talk to outstanding employees in the company. Employees who deliver positive experiences often have a good eye for talented people like them. They can say which candidate fits the standards and who they will be happy to work with.

In every assessment tool, pay close attention to the following service traits:

- A smiling voice, conversation style and concise speech.
- Attentiveness.
- Empathy and kindness.
- Positive energy and enthusiasm.
- Being creative and working under pressure.
- Passionate about providing service.
- Innovative service thinking.

Each candidate should receive a score from 1 to 100 on each selection tool used. The scores need to be documented and kept in the candidate's file. These scores are going to be important when we discuss how to evaluate the effectiveness of the selection process.

An Interesting Fact

Service providers' customer orientation positively impacts customer responses, such as likely to purchase from that company in the future, loyalty, and word-of-mouth. This improves the performance of the company.

Customer orientation positively influences job satisfaction, commitment, as well as organizational citizenship behaviors. It enhances service employees' psychological welfare in addition to being good for business [4].

An experience selection process

HR that expects candidates who are hired to provide experiences must turn the selection process into a positive experience. It must show candidates that everything revolves around the customer.

Whether the selection is made on a computer online or face-to-face, the company's customer-centric vision and values are on forms, website, and interview room. Beyond that, there are several actions that create a positive perception among candidates:

- The candidate is personally greeted by name.
- Help is available for the candidate anytime during the process.
- The interaction starts at the scheduled time.
- Any delay in the selection process is communicated to the candidate with an apology and length of delay.
- Candidates who weren't hired receive an explanation why, helping them get better for future selection processes.

A positive selection process leads candidates to have a positive perception of the company and be enthusiastic to work for it. Even those who don't get the job might praise the company, and encourage others to apply there for a job. Candidates are also potential customers of the brand. They might not get the job, but they might want to buy what the company is selling. That is a win-win situation.

Step 3: Evaluating the effectiveness of the service-oriented selection process

Every company has a selection process. A simple question arises: How good is the selection process? To answer this question, it has to be broken down into two questions:

Question 1: Is the selection process effective — does it consistently yield people who perform at the company's service standards and deliver great experiences?

Question 2: Is the selection process efficient — do candidates go through selection steps with minimum wasted effort, time, or expense?

Answers to these two questions require the company to analyze the selection process from start to finish. The answers should be collected from three different sources — candidates, employees, and managers. Here is a more in-depth look at each question.

Question 1: Is the selection process effective?

The selection effectiveness can be evaluated on five major aspects:

- **Fit with the job** — A month after a person was hired, a manager must ask themselves "would I rehire that person?" In that time frame, the manager has seen the new person in action and can assess whether the hiring decision was the correct one.
- **Fit with colleagues** — After a couple of weeks on the job, the team members should evaluate the new people. Did they embrace the company's culture and values? Are they getting along with other people? Are they customer- and service-oriented?
- **Fit with customers** — Do customers served by the new hire enjoy the interactions? What do they say about them? What is their customer satisfaction score?
- **Fit with performance standards** — What is the new hire's productivity and internal customer service level after two or three months? Does the new hire adhere to the company's standards, "Carry his or her own weight", and doesn't become a burden to others?
- **Fit with the company** — Last but not least, do the new hires have a positive feeling about their job, colleagues, managers, and customers? Do they feel they are in a good place and fit right in? Are they happy? Do they see themselves staying with the company for the long haul?

After collecting the information above, correlate it with the candidate's scores given through the selection process. An effective selection system results in high, positive correlations. Low correlations means the scores given throughout the hiring process don't predict the candidate's actual fit at work. This makes the selection process fruitless. All in all, everyone wants to see that the hires today are better than hires in the past.

Question 2: Is the selection process efficient?

An efficient selection process achieves maximum results with minimum waste. The selection efficiency can be evaluated by asking the entities who were part of the process — HR department, managers, employees, and candidates who went through the process — the following questions:

- Was the selection process a positive experience?
- Was the process smooth, without problems or mistakes? If not, what went wrong?
- Was the process draining? If yes, why?
- What would you have done differently in the selection process?
- Can the selection process be improved by technology?
- Would you recommend the company to your friends?

The answers will help identify potential flaws in the process and allow the company to fix them. Constantly improving the process, making it better, faster, and cheaper.

Selecting the right people is the first step. Next, the company has to make sure new hires can deliver great experiences. That requires training and development.

Train and Develop for Xperiences

Customers are becoming savvier and more knowledgeable. They come prepared for the encounter by doing online research about the company's products, services, price options, as well as its competitors. They challenge employees' knowledge and abilities with smart questions and special requests. Service training is the best tool to help employees stay ahead of customers, and the company ahead of the competition.

Companies are sometimes hesitant to provide extensive training because of the cost associated with it. Training is expensive, but what is the alternative? Training customer-facing employees and seeing them leave the company is disappointing. Resources are wasted and frustrations mount. Not training them and seeing them stay, is much worse. Service providers don't have the necessary capabilities and they drive customers away. Training should be looked at as an investment. Done right, training provides high returns on such an investment.

Companies delivering extensive and effective service training enjoy three major positive outcomes.

1. **Employees' expertism** — Employees improve their skills and/or acquire new ones which help them have better interactions with customers. They grow in their job, maximize their potential, and thus become more motivated and engaged, which ultimately reduces turnover.
2. **Customers' engagement** — Customers enjoy the benefits of employees' expanded skillset. Their issues are resolved faster and they feel cared for, appreciated, and respected. This raises customer satisfaction and loyalty.
3. **Company's success** — The company achieves higher profits. People are more productive, additional customers are acquired, sales are improved, and costs are reduced. Consequently, the company's brand reputation strengthens.

Effective training ensures service providers across the company deliver consistent service. Different employees with different knowledge, experiences, and background come to the company. It's a diverse group. Training provides everyone a similar skillset that gets them to perform on a certain standard which eliminates much of the variance in actions. Employees aren't robots and variance in the level of service exists. But as long as the variance is narrow and reasonable, customers accept it. An effective training for experiences includes three key steps:

Step 1: Service competencies needs assessment → Step 2: Training for service competencies → Step 3: Evaluating the training effectiveness

Step 1: Service competencies needs assessment

Needs assessment helps identify the competencies and behaviors that employees need to deliver experiences now and in the future. Needs assessment should be done on three levels:

The organizational level — Understanding needs on the company-wide level. This is done by answering questions like:

- Which department or branch needs which competencies to serve their customers both internally and externally?
- Which competencies will be needed with changes in customers' expectations, competition, the economy, and workforce demographics?
- What is the most effective training method for teaching each competency?

The job position level — Understanding needs on the task-function level. This is done by asking questions like:

- Which competencies are required to fulfill key assignments and duties as well as delivering great service in each service position?
- Should the training be given based on tenure at the position, or the service provider's readiness for the training?

The individual level — Understanding the needs at a person level. This is done by asking questions like:

- What does each individual need to maximize their potential and deliver exceptional experience?
- What are the learning styles of each individual? What kind of training fits each individual?
- What motivates service providers to improve themselves?

An accurate needs assessment provides the foundation for designing an effective service competencies training program.

Step 2: Training for service competencies

The company's approach to training influences people's perception of the company's seriousness about service. New hires who receive extensive training before starting the job realize that the company's high level of service standards is real, no compromising is done, and that the company puts the necessary effort to make sure everyone is a professional experience provider. Tenured employees who receive constant training to improve their skillset perceive the company in a positive light. Seeing that the company invests in their development causes them to invest back by providing high quality service. Overall, training everyone in the company for service competencies sends a clear message about the importance of delivering experiences in any job. There are several important points to consider when training new and existing employees.

Training new service providers

Training new employees for service competencies takes time and requires substantial investment. That is a necessary and sound investment. In-depth, effective training eliminates many of the unacceptable mistakes that new employees make that can substantially hurt customers. Singapore Airlines provides several months of initial training to its flight attendants. This is a much lengthy training program than those of its competitors. The lengthy training assures that every new employee can deliver a high quality experience from day one, such that customers will have a difficult time telling the difference between a new employee and a veteran one.

Effective training for new employees is a confidence booster. They feel capable performing their tasks on a high level and interact effectively with customers. That creates a comfort level that is very important in the early stages of employment.

Training new employees can also be used as another screening tool. What is the new hires' reaction to the training? Employees who dismiss the learning sessions, don't pay attention, disrupt the training, or just can't keep up, raise a red flag. These are indicators that maybe something was missed in the selection process and the wrong person was hired. This allows the company to part ways with them and fix the selection mistake before substantial harm occurs.

Training existing service providers

Training existing employees is a marathon not a sprint. Throughout the duration of people's tenure with the company, there is always room to develop new abilities and improve, upgrade, and polish existing competencies. It constantly improves performance. For the training to have both immediate and lasting value, the following guidelines should be followed:

Personalizing the training — Training can be done in a variety of ways (Computer, colleagues, manager, etc.) and in different places (Classroom, self-learning on a computer, peer learning on the job, etc.) with various methods (Text, video, discussion, role-playing, etc.). The training program must be flexible enough for each individual to choose the best combination of method, time, and place for training. Fitting the training for each individual makes it more effective and yields better results.

Making the training fit people's jobs — The closer the training is to mimicking skills and abilities needed for the job, the more people will listen and learn. People who see that the training helps them do their job better, see it as added incentive to learn. This makes the training more effective.

Creating cross-departmental training groups — By assembling people from different departments, they don't just learn but also interact with each other. They build relationships and study how to improve inter-departmental cooperation. The training should include sharing service knowledge, success stories, and best practices in handling service failure. This is a great way to do a "brain storming" session to come up with new ways or improve current processes and deliver better service and more memorable experiences.

A training program can't be static. It has to adapt and transform. It has to be dynamic enough to fit different situations, trainees' profiles, technology, uncertain business environment, and other changes. An evaluation of the training process enables the company to see what works and what doesn't, making it do the necessary changes.

Step 3: Evaluating the service competencies training effectiveness

Service training that helps employees deliver better experiences is priceless while training that doesn't bring such benefits, is just a waste of resources. An evaluation of the training from start to finish based on feedback from all sources involved in the process can determine if the training results were positive or negative. Two important facets should be evaluated:

The training outcome — This facet checks if people's service performance was improved. The evaluation should look at people's service performance before the training and in periodic intervals for three months after the training is done. Questions that can help evaluate the performance include: Was the purpose or goals of the training achieved? Did customers' ratings for trained employees rise? Did productivity improve? Were there less mistakes made? Are customers more satisfied with the company?

The training process — This facet checks the efficiency and effectiveness of the training procedure. Ask trainers and trainees what worked well during the training and what didn't. When training is done on a computer, technology can monitor and evaluate the process. Question that can help evaluate the process include: Were the right methods used to teach the material? Was there too much or not enough time for certain topics? Was the training moving along smoothly or were there bumps along the way? Was there time to ask questions or practice the material? Are the best employees happy with the training process?

The evaluation of the training effectiveness helps the company optimize the process. A better process advances people service skills and helps the company achieve better results.

A successful training and development process yields people with the necessary service competencies (Figure 9.4). The next step is to make sure they use those competencies consistently over time. That requires compensating for service achievements.

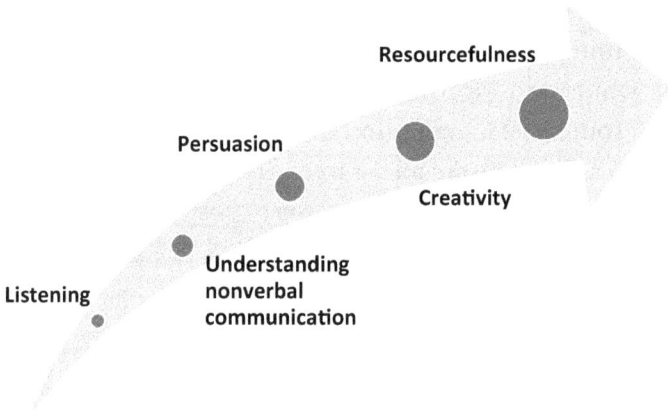

Figure 9.4. Five Soft Skills for Delivering Better Experiences

Compensate Service Achievements

The level of compensation shows how important someone is to the company. High compensation means important and contributes to its success. Low compensation means inessential and replaceable. Many organizations still underappreciate the impact that service providers have on success and thus provide them with low compensation.

A customer-facing position is a difficult job to perform — dealing with customers' needs, wants, and sometimes negative behavior.

While maintaining a friendly, attentive and kind conduct, day-in and day-out.

Compensation is the way for companies to say thank you, to appreciate and applaud employees for their hard work and dedication to providing experiences. Substantial rewards are loud applause that motivate people to continue and repeat the behaviors and actions that led to the applause. Low rewards are no applause, which dramatically reduces motivation to do the job and serve customers.

After investing time and effort in selecting service-oriented employees and training them to deliver great experiences, it only makes sense to build a compensation system that motivates people to deliver those experiences consistently over time. Such a system is composed of three steps:

Step 1: Experience performance appraisal

Experience performance appraisal is a process whereby employees' ability to deliver great experiences to customers is evaluated and documented. It's what gets praised, gets noticed, and people focus their effort on it. Thus, companies that want experiences should put experiences (External as well as internal) front and center in the performance appraisal.

An effective appraisal process helps achieve three main objectives:

- Determine each person's level of service performance.
- Identify areas of service strength that need to be enhanced and weakness needed to be developed.
- Uncover potential for future service role growth.

There are several themes that companies must get right to make sure people trust the performance appraisal and embrace it. Here are a few of them:

Make it simple — Customer experience is composed of many dimensions. To make the appraisal process simple, it should include only a handful of critical experience metrics. The limited number makes it simple for people to follow and understand how they are appraised. It helps to set simple guidelines and specific achievement targets needed to get the compensation. For example, reaching level X on metric Y will result in compensation Z. There might be a need to establish targets not only at the individual level but also at the team, branch, and even organizational level.

Make it actionable — People need to feel they can influence the set performance appraisal metrics. They need to see that investing time and effort on their part yields better experience metrics which, in turn, triggers better rewards. The reward should increase with every new milestone reached. The harder they work, the higher the rewards. That motivates them to put forward extra effort. It's important to listen to employees' grievances with the metrics and make the necessary adjustments when possible. Listening to them raises their commitment to the appraisal process which makes it simpler to implement.

Make it fair — A fair appraisal system evaluates every employee in the company on the same experience metrics, sets the same targets for everyone, the same level of rewards when reaching those targets. The best service performer gets the highest appraisal. That might sound simple but preferential treatment, playing favorites, and organizational politics often lead to unfair results. Transparency is crucial. Employees know who the best service performers are. If they see them receiving the highest appraisal, they believe the system is fair.

A fair system leads employees to trust it. Otherwise, it quickly alienates them. Raising the targets every year while keeping the same compensation is unfair. Employees shouldn't work harder for the same level of compensation. Not telling employees if they are competing against themselves or a certain customer benchmark is also unfair and leads to mistrust.

Make it 360-degree — To get the best, most comprehensive appraisal, performance data should be collected from different sources — customers, colleagues, managers, and others. Merging the information from the different sources provides a complete, accurate, and less biased picture of each individual service performance.

Make it competitive — Competition can lead to positive outcomes as well as negative ones. Friendly competition between employees is positive because it drives everyone to be the best, be creative, and think outside the box. Making the competition on-going the extra mile, challenging the status quo, or raising service innovative ideas is also a positive competition because it makes everyone better. However, cut-throat competition where one person's gain comes on the back of another, leads to negative and unnecessary outcomes.

Make it consistent — A consistent performance appraisal leads to certainty which leads to calmness. Employees expect to be evaluated the same way, time after time. They don't like to see major changes or a focus shift from one thing to another. It confuses them and they lose focus. Consistency outlines the playing field and the rules. Once all the parameters are known and constant, people feel they can "play" the game and succeed.

An appraisal that adheres to the guidelines outlined above accurately describes each employee level of performance down to a tee. It ranks all employees from best to lowest, with usually little argument. Everything is documented and transparent for everyone to see. Once the appraisal is done, the next step is to provide experience rewards.

Step 2: Rewarding the delivery of experiences

Rewards are like a big spotlight. What gets rewarded gets the spotlight. What gets the spotlight gets people's attention and consequently gets done. Companies that want great experiences should put a big spotlight on it by providing handsome rewards for those who deliver it. A meager reward states that experiences aren't that important, despite what the vision statement proclaims or what the upper management states.

Rewards are a tool to acknowledge the employees' value to the company and their service achievements. It's praising them for doing great work, celebrating their service success, and showing appreciation and caring. Rewards are the company's applause to people providing great experiences to customers. Loud applause (substantial rewards) motivates people to overcome significant challenge at work and continue to provide great service. Mute applause (modest rewards) leads employees to do the bare minimum.

When it comes to rewarding experiences, more is better than less, especially for high performers. Rewards give people a sense of accomplishment and gratitude from the company. Capping rewards leads to employees capping their performance, matching the reward. A dollar saved on lower compensation today, will often cause the company to lose many dollars on customer dissatisfaction in the future. What is the level of service provided by underpaid and unappreciated employees? The answer is the reason for handsomely rewarding service providers.

There is no need to over-compensate, but it's definitely in the best interest of the company to give the highest compensation in the marketplace. That increases people's self-worth, and they repay the company by doing quality work and being loyal. This reduces the considerable costs associated with replacing the service provider. To establish an effective rewards program, three themes should be followed.

Personalized reward — Compensation has maximum influence when the right reward is provided to the right employee, at the right time. By matching the reward — monetary and non-monetary, to each employee's intrinsic needs, life events, hobbies, limitations, etc., an optimum level of employee delight and engagement is achieved. Yes, a small, personalized reward can have a more long-lasting effect than an extravagant reward that everyone receives.

People reward people — Empower employees to nominate their colleagues for reward over exceptional service performance. HR and managers can't always see what employees are doing and the achievements they reach. By letting people praise and cheer each other, important achievements don't fall through the cracks and a positive culture of teamwork rises which motivates people to work better together. That improves cooperation and the willingness to provide high quality service. A great example is a monthly "Praise meeting" in which people's names are called, they stand up and receive praise from their colleagues. Everyone cheers. It's an inspiring event for everyone. People love this meeting and eagerly await it.

Changing rewards — When a reward is given, people are excited. The second time they get it, the excitement subsides. With every usage of the same reward, the excitement is diminished. Using different bonuses and constantly changing them keeps the element of surprise. To get back the excitement from rewards, there is a full array of bonuses that can be used. There are ways to compensate today that didn't exist ten and fifteen years ago. Continually surprising people with rewards isn't easy, but the benefits are worth the effort.

Every company rewards its employees. But is the reward effective in making sure experiences are delivered consistently? To answer this question, there is a need to evaluate the effectiveness of the experience rewards program.

Step 3: Evaluating the effectiveness of experience rewards

Rewards represent a substantial cost for companies. Rewards that motivate employees to deliver exceptional experiences are an investment worth making. Rewards that have marginal or no influence on employees' actions or service performance are pointless. Evaluating the rewards system is the way to know how good it is. An effective system achieves the following outcomes:

1. Drives people to provide great experiences.
2. Eliminates unwanted activities, actions and behaviors.
3. Reinforces constant learning and improving service skills and experience abilities.
4. Gets everyone to focus on and follow the company's customer-oriented vision, strategy and core values.
5. Challenges people to go the extra mile for customers.
6. Keeps high service performers happy, motivated, and engaged.
7. Creates a healthy and friendly competition among people within the company that pushes them to perform on a higher level.
8. Acts as a magnet that attracts exceptional service providers from other companies.

A reward models future performance and not just acknowledges past performance. The information collected above can be used to adjust and improve the rewards process so it stays effective over time. This eliminates any mishap in the rewards process that can have a negative influence on employees' confidence or performance.

Service providers need to get a lot of things right in order to delight customers. Their job is difficult, stressful, and challenging. Celebrating, recognizing, and rewarding their effort helps them overcome those difficulties and perform to the best of their abilities. This results in higher performance and quality of service. It doesn't get any simpler than that.

Conclusion

HR meets everyone in the company and thus plays a vital role in achieving the company's strategic service goals and implementing the service-oriented culture. It influences who gets hired, determines their skillset and level and engagement, and thus determines their level of service performance. By managing its own practices in a customer-oriented way, HR can get everyone moving together, in lockstep, concentrating their efforts on making customers happy.

HR has to be active. It has to constantly analyze its practices and adapt them to the rapid pace of the business environment. Also, it has to think beyond the here and now; be aware of future trends and make the necessary preparations.

References

[1] Sorenson, S. (2013). How Employee Engagement Drives Growth. Available at https://www.gallup.com/workplace/236927/employee-engagement-drives-growth.aspx

[2] Olga, Provide Support Blog (2015). Customer Service Staff Turnover. The Real Cost. Available at https://www.providesupport.com/blog/customer-service-staff-turnover-the-real-cost-infographics/

[3] Expert Rating (2022). Customer Service Aptitude Test. Available at https://www.expertratinginc.com/testsyllabus.aspx?examid=7135&catid=239

[4] Shega, T.M. (2013). Using Personality Traits to Select Customer-Oriented Security Guards. Cornerstone, Minnesota State University. Available at https://cornerstone.lib.mnsu.edu/cgi/viewcontent.cgi?article=1166&context=etds

Part 3

Deliver the Xperience

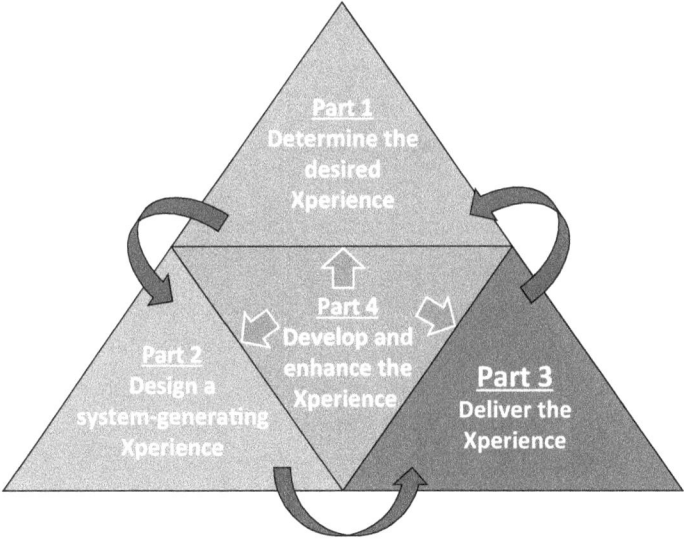

The 4D Xperience Model

When thinking about delivering experiences, a common question arises: Should technology or people be used to serve customers?

Companies struggle to answer this question. On one side, for decades, humans were the dominant customers' servers. The organization's system, procedures and processes were built for human service. On the other side, advanced technology changes everything and hypnotizes companies. Serving customers through technology is faster, more precise, more consistent, can deliver human-like service, and is cheaper.

To answer the question above, another, more fundamental question should be asked; a question that was asked in lecture three: What do customers want? What makes their life easier? Simpler? More convenient?

Choosing technology to replace people or having people instead of technology isn't the proper frame of mind. As is often the case in life, the choice isn't one or the other, but rather a combination. The right combination; a hybrid, where technology and humans work hand-in-hand, each playing to their relative strengths.

Customers may sometimes choose technology (they need something fast) and sometimes human (they need someone to take ownership, responsibility, while reassuring that "everything will be fine"). They get to choose. The company develops both and doesn't prefer one over the other, allowing customers to switch seamlessly between the two.

In the end, delivering an experience is about people and technology "rowing the boat" together, in harmony, toward offering customers rich, personalized experiences.

Lectures 10 and 11 outline how technology and humans should operate to deliver desired experiences.

Lecture 10

Autonomous Xperience: Technology Serving People

"Technology is a useful servant but a dangerous master."

Christian Lous Lange, Historian

Customers can get what they need from companies in two avenues: humans (people serve customers), or technology (people serve themselves autonomously). In the past, autonomous service (i.e., self-service) was a limited option and most of the service was received from humans. Now, it's the opposite. Most interactions with companies occur through self-service. People are replaced by websites, kiosks, and other smart machines. That isn't a bad thing. Customers aren't just ready for self-service; almost 70% of them actually prefer to use it over human support [1]. Companies without an effective self-service portal might alienate customers, especially young ones.

Self-service makes sense if customers are able to get what they need in a fast, easy, and enjoyable way. Would a customer rather wait in line to get what they need when the same result can be achieved through a kiosk or website with no wait? This is a primary reason for customer migration away from traditional service channels such as phone or face-to-face, towards autonomous options.

An Interesting Fact

More than 70% of customers think self-service is the fastest and easiest way to handle support issues.

Moreover, 40% of customers who contacted call centers have already looked for an answer via self-service options but didn't find one and were forced to call [2].

When customers have an issue, immediate help is expected. Not tomorrow when the company opens its doors. Self-service is the only channel that can consistently offer 24/7/365 service available to every customer, allowing them to solve issues on their own right away, without assistance from the company. Customers perform the service representative's job while using an automated platform.

An effective self-service leads to a win-win situation for both customers and companies. It enables customers to do things on their own time and at their own pace, giving them a sense of accomplishment and pride when they successfully achieve the result. Granting the customer a powerful positive feeling that causes them to use the autonomous option again in the future.

The win for companies is the cost reduction. Serving customers through self-service costs the company as much as ten dollars less per interaction [3]. Self-service dramatically decreases the workload on employees. It's estimated that 60% of customer service calls are requests for assistance with common, uncomplicated tasks that can be avoided with self-service [4]. An effective self-service increases customer satisfaction, retention, and lowers companies' overall marketing costs [5].

Offering customers the right sequence of service options looks like this:

Companies are spending time, energy, and money on improving, managing, and measuring channels in which customers get service from people (Talk-service). Even though it isn't the customer's first choice and it's the company's most expensive channel. That makes little sense. Upgrading the self-service portal and delivering a great autonomous experience makes more sense and leads to better results.

Guidelines for Designing Exceptional Autonomous Experience (AE)

Designing a great autonomous experience is a challenge. A machine has to replace the human that customers are so used to. Machines can't be kind, understand nuances, read between the lines, or provide clarifications or reassuring words when the customer needs it most of all.

When designing an autonomous self-service portal, the average customer should be the compass — he or she isn't an expert, they are extremely busy and not willing to put effort into it. The portal should look, feel, and be built accordingly (Figure 10.1).

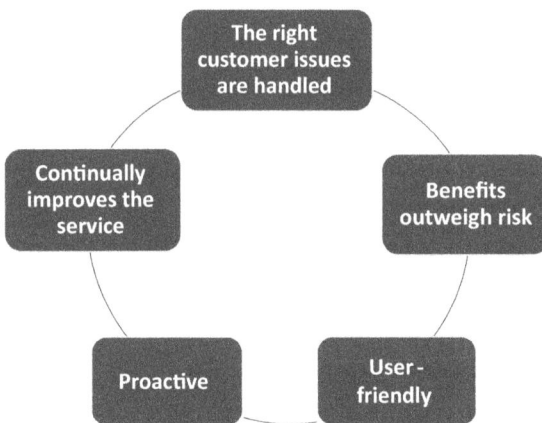

Figure 10.1. The Elements of An Exceptional Autonomous Experience

Here is a more in-depth look at the different elements presented in Figure 10.1.

The right customer issues are handled — While self-service is an effective portal, it isn't a magic wand. Like every tool that exists, it does certain things very well and other things not as good. Thus, certain issues can be solved through self-service while others can't. Self-service thrives on handling simpler tasks to moderate service issues. Complicated issues should mostly be dealt with by humans over the phone or face-to face. Trying to use the self-service to deal with complicated issues will probably result in errors, misunderstandings, customer dissatisfaction, and higher costs.

Simple, moderate, and complex issues are subjective terms. Following customers through their self-service journey can help companies see and understand customers' frame of mind, the difficulties they face, their limitations, and what they are willing and unwilling to do when using self-service. This information helps decipher in which cases the customer can reach a resolution by themselves and in which they can't and need human help. Obviously, some customers have more technical know-how to use self-service portals, and some are unable or unwilling to do so. Those who are unable shouldn't be penalized for their decision and should get connected to human assistance.

Benefits outweigh risk — Customers feel safer receiving service from humans. They will use self-service if the perceived risk is limited, while the perceived benefits must be substantial. In other words, the company has to achieve the right balance between what customers give when using the portal and what they get in return. Customers give time and effort by doing all the work themselves. In return, they should get the service at their own convenience, flawlessly.

Companies that want customers to do more complicated tasks autonomously that require more effort should be ready to provide compensation in a form of a discount or other reward in return. This maintains the value proposition.

In using self-service, customers do all the work. Service providers receive training from the company to do their job. If customers are expected to replace service providers, they should also get training on how to effectively use the self-service portal. Enabling them to do things autonomously and boosts their confidence that they will be successful.

Training doesn't just help customers use the portal effectively, it also demonstrates a dedication from the company to their success. That is a powerful message to customers, improving trust in the company.

User-friendly — The self-service portal should be easy to learn and simple to use. This requires the company to ensure that the portal is:

- Visually appealing.
- Organized and categorized intuitively.
- Accessible to individuals with disabilities.
- Streamlined, easy to navigate, and with effective search functionality.
- Reliable and safe. Data confidentiality is kept, and information is protected.
- Optimized content for any device.

Proactive — An effective self-service portal offers contextual information during the customer's journey rather than merely letting customers find it themselves. It guides customers to the next best steps to take in their journey, based on their preference, behavior, nature of the query, and goals. It offers ideas and suggestions to help customers get the best possible option (offering an option not taken into account) and prevents them from making mistakes (not letting customers press the wrong buttons).

Continually improves the service — Self-service portals can't be stagnant. An effective portal goes through constant refinement and evolution to improve the customer experience. When customers use self-service, they leave a trail of data. Every action can be observed — every keystroke, every button pressed, and every mistake made. Companies that monitor, review, and analyze those actions can develop a better understanding of customer behavior. Then, use the insights to perform incremental tweaking that's needed to improve the customer experience.

Characteristics of an Exceptional AE

When it comes to self-service, the key word is effort. The best predictor of exceptional AE is how much effort customers put forward to use the portal. Minimal effort means a great experience while substantial effort means poor experience. Here are several characteristics of an impeccable self-service portal that delivers exceptional experiences.

Simplicity — Simple is always better than complicated. Simple helps customers overcome a fear they have regarding the usage of self-service technology. It eliminates confusion and helps overcome lack of self-efficacy and perceived risk of the portal. When all fears are muted, the core advantages and strengths stand out and the chances of using the portal are higher. Simple has to be on a customer's first trail. Many customers won't give a second chance to self-service even after the company invested resources and dramatically simplified the portal.

When it comes to simplicity, companies have a dilemma. On one hand, making it simpler and easier for customers invariably requires the organization to work hard and it doesn't come cheap. Furthermore, managing and maintaining simplicity consistently takes even more resources. On the other hand, providing customers with a complex AE is simple and easy for the organization to implement, but it frustrates customers. Consequently, designing and implementing a simple AE leads to a win-win situation that is worth the effort and cost.

Convenience — The concept of self-service automatically offers convenience to customers. It's constantly accessible and can fit well with their needs, activities, and plans. There is no need to adhere to certain opening hours, standing in line, or even leaving the house. Also, customers get everything they need in one place. Reducing the hassle to go to several places.

Convenience is subjective. The customer, not the company, determines if something is convenient. When a customer doesn't perceive something as convenient, then it isn't. Convenience is also relative. Customers compare between companies they receive service from whether in the same or different industry. Customers can state "I want a company X kind of convenience." Finally, convenience can change over time. What customers have deemed comfortable in the past, might be regarded today as inconvenient.

Control — People want and like to be in control. The self-service portal gives customers complete control. They decide when to use the portal, how to use it, and what to do. A liquor store offered its customers to order on-line for delivery. That led to an interesting trend. Customers started buying wines with brand names that are difficult to pronounce. They didn't ask salespeople for those brands, not wanting to be embarrassed by pronouncing the name wrong. Once they were on-line and in control, they bought those brands.

Companies can give customers control by empowering them to make decisions when using the portal. They can offer customers several possible options and let them choose. For example, letting a customer choose their own seat on the plane or in a restaurant feels powerful. The company can provide suggestions along the way but no restrictions or limitations that forces customers to choose what the company wants.

As customers have more experience using the self-service, they become sort of experts. As customers know more, they feel a sense of control and relish the opportunity to do more and handle extra responsibility. The company can use their expertise to teach them about features in the portal they aren't aware of, or a new feature that is introduced. This entices them to use the portal more. The company can even go a step further and ask some veteran customers for their opinion on how to improve the portal. Making them feel in control over future changes on the portal. That is an advanced dimension of control.

Speed — We live in a high-speed internet world. That means warp speed — fast, faster, fastest. Time is the most precious, perishable resource that people have. Any wait is considered by customers as a waste of time. Anything that saves time is valuable and desirable. Self-service allows customers to quickly get what they need without the waiting and that makes it valuable.

To stay as a desirable option, self-service has to constantly become more efficient, improve its speed, and get customers through the portal as fast as possible — faster than other service channels. If customers think there is no substantial difference in speed between human service and self-service, they will choose human more often than not.

The perception of fast can change with time. What was considered fast a year ago might be considered not so fast and even slow tomorrow. Slow companies quickly lose to competition and become irrelevant. In trying to increase speed, it's important to keep in mind that it can't come on the expense of quality, accuracy, convenience, etc.

Information — Customers need the right information to be able to serve themselves. The right information checks all the following aspects:

- **Trustworthy** — No bias or hidden agenda.
- **Reliable** — Accurate, up-to-date content with no errors or out-dated data.
- **Relevant and complete** — Provides all the content needed for the issue at hand.
- **Timely** — Given at the right time during the process.
- **Focused** — Short, brief, straight to the point with no lengthy explanations (Customers should have the option to elaborate more on each topic).

- **Clear and understandable** — Style, language, sentence structure, terms, and jargons should adhere to customers. No house terminology or tech-speak.

The information that customers need rarely resides in a single repository or knowledge base. It's created, shared, and stored across platforms, departments, databases, both on the premises and in the cloud. To provide customers with the right information, there has to be sharing of information throughout the organization. This means taking the collective knowledge and turning it into productive content that customers can read and use. With so much information, an effective search option should be provided, enabling customers to quickly find the needed information. Sounds easy? Most customers are annoyed with the search field found in the self-service portals [6].

Delivering information through the portal can happen in a variety of ways — FAQ (Frequently Asked Questions), documents, pictures, screenshots, videos, articles, etc. Each way has its pros and cons. Companies should learn which way can best be used to deliver which information and work accordingly.

Personalization — The self-service portal has to be flexible enough to adjust and deal with different customers. As customers use the portal, more information is collected from them. That information is then used to improve the experience every time they enter the portal.

The system can identify them and customize a path that best fits that customer usage history. Same issue, same path. If it's a different issue, give customers the path that best fits their profile and explain why that path is the best one and then provide advice along the usage.

Consistency — An answer that a customer receives on the self-service portal has to be the same answer the customer would have gotten if they talked to a service provider. This is crucial. If a customer got one answer from self-service and a different one from the representative, that will lead to uncertainty and mistrust. The customer is going to wonder which answer is better and why is there a discrepancy. That usually causes customers to choose a human next time they make contact. A poor result for both sides.

A Great Example — Amazon

Amazon has built Amazon Go, a convenience store that has no registers or cashiers. A customer can walk in, pick out what they want, and walk out. Amazon calls it a "just walk out" shopping experience.

The customer enters the store, scans their Amazon Go App and starts collecting items. The store uses technologies such as computer vision, sensor fusion, and deep learning to detect the product put in the basket or returned to the shelves and keep track of them in the virtual cart.

When the customer leaves, the products are added up, the Amazon account is charged, and the receipt is sent online. Simple, convenient, fast, and personalized.

Self-service portals are advancing rapidly and becoming more and more intelligent. Those portals are known as Artificial Intelligence (AI) and Augmented Reality (AR). These two technologies broaden the horizons of self-service capabilities, providing resourceful and proactive solutions relevant to a vast array of issues and much broader audiences. Let's take a closer look at these technologies.

Intelligent Self-Service: Enhancing AE Through AI and AR

No matter how good the self-service portals are, customers will have questions, encounter problems, or make mistakes. They will require assistance. The common practice is to transfer the customer to a service provider. But having a human assistant defeats the purpose of self-service. Artificial intelligence (AI) and augmented reality (AR) can help customers get the solution they need without leaving

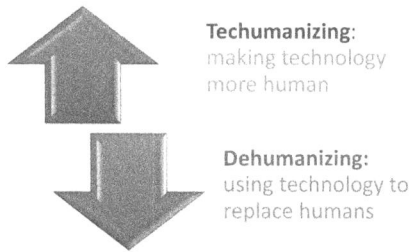

Figure 10.2. Humanizing Technology

the portal or talking to a human (Figure 10.2). AI and AR are revolutionizing the service landscape by providing innovative, groundbreaking capabilities that open service options that never existed in self-service. This makes the experience more interactive and valuable for customers.

An Interesting Fact

It is suggested that by 2025, AI will power 95% of all customer interactions [7].

About 79% of customers, especially those ages 13–17 of Gen Z, are more likely to visit stores that offer interactive AI and VR experience that helps customize the products and accurately predict what they need [8].

AI and AR make self-service smoother and easier to use. They change the way customers view self-service, making them realize that talking to a human is becoming unnecessary. Let's take a closer look at the advantages of each of these technologies.

AI-powered self-service

AI is a learning algorithm aimed at simulating human intelligence and actions during the self-service encounter. The platform absorbs data and information from any source available — the company itself, companies in the same industry around the globe, relevant publishing research, etc. The more information, the better the platform can learn and understand every possible outcome that can happen during the encounter.

The AI takes all the input, sorts it out, classifies it into categories, and looks for correlations and causation within the data. It understands what leads to a positive or a negative outcome, or which action or behavior from one side leads to positive and negative actions and reactions from the other side.

Once AI learns how people behave in each situation, what worked and what failed, it can start to understand how to operate effectively and serve customers. Over time, AI learns more, understands more, and can identify the best possible solution for each issue that customers face. Combining that with the customer's profile and usage history, AI can personalize the offering and provide relevant choices for each individual customer. Every incremental encounter, whether a success or a failure, improves the AI abilities, reduces possible mistakes, and thus improves the overall customer experience.

An Interesting Fact

Research shows that virtual assistants reduce product return across industries by 17% and other key performance indicators by 20%–40% after eighteen months [9].

AI adds several more advantages to the self-service portal:

Ready to help — AI is like a chaperone. It accompanies and supervises the customer along the journey, but behind the scenes. Always there, ready to guide, but only intervenes when the customer is unsure, hesitant, or asks for help. By following the customer, AI already knows everything — what the customer wants, what was chosen from the menu, etc. There is no need for the customer to explain what they did. They just need to say what is necessary at that moment and the AI will offer the possible options. That makes the customer's life much easier with no wasted effort or being irritated with the need to repeat information. This allows a quick resolution to the issue at hand and quickly gets the customer what they need.

Indicate improvement opportunities — By constantly monitoring the customer journey, AI can detect where customers showed hesitancy, had to back track, or clicked on the wrong button. Over time and with tremendous amount of data, AI can identify systemic flaws and find ineffective processes and vulnerabilities in the self-service portal. It can offer ideas why they happened and even pinpoint the origin of the problem, thereby showing what has to be improved. This allows the company to fix the right things quickly.

When a new feature is offered through the self-service portal, AI can be of help. It can follow the customer's usage of the new feature. How many times did the customers use it, when, how long it took, and how many reused it? This is a critical information in understanding if the new feature is popular, if any change is needed, or maybe it should be discarded altogether.

Predicting behavior — Customers tend to have patterns. They ask similar questions, encounter similar difficulties, and follow a similar path. AI can learn those patterns, choices, and activities, and produce useful insights that delve into what happened and provide an accurate guess as to the next action the customers will take. This allows AI to offer customers something they need before they asked for it, creating a positive surprise and a WOW moment.

AI can flag customers who act in a way that leads to them leaving the company, allowing the company to interact with each of those customers and reduce churn. AI can also analyze questions that customers ask and comments they make to uncover hidden wishes. This provides the company with an opportunity to fill those needs in the future and create additional value.

Completely autonomous service — With virtual assistants, AI self-service is very close to becoming fully autonomous. The customer will say what they want or need and the voice-activated AI will do everything. In rare instances where a new request was never heard before or the request is too complex for the AI to understand, it will ask clarifying questions and request additional data. The AI is going to try and figure out what the new information means. It will browse for options, select and furnish appropriate answers or steps that might be related. The process might be longer and the customer might do some of the work but the AI is at their side, guiding them through every step making the overall, somewhat complicated experience a positive one.

All in all, AI makes the self-service portal more flawless, effortless, and personalized. It optimizes the customer experience and constantly improves upon it, leading customers to use the portal more often and reduce to a minimum the need for human help.

AR-powered self-service

AR is a technology that seamlessly bridges the physical and virtual worlds. As such, it enables companies to integrate the online (virtual world) and offline (physical world). Customers receive an interactive digital experience that dramatically helps them serve themselves. The transformation and advancement of the customer journey by AR is so impressive that more than 70% of best-in-class service organizations utilize it, compared to their peers [10].

AR uses immersive 3D visuals that overlay images onto physical objects and environment via mobile devices. Visual images, compared to auditory communication, help customers be more accurate in what they do, make better decisions, and avoid mistakes. This upgrades the self-service experience.

A Good Example — IKEA

The company is using AR to help customers envision how different furnitures will look inside their homes. Customers look through an online catalog, select an item they want to preview, then use their smart device camera to display the product at any place in their home (bathroom, living room, etc.)

With AR, customers can be more confident in their buying decision. Uplifting their satisfaction while reducing buyers' remorse and return rate to a minimum.

AR improves the self-service experience in two additional ways:

Remove uncertainty — When customers go to buy something online, imagination plays a major role. They have to envision things: Will this dishwasher fit in my kitchen? How will the device look outside the box? How will an article of cloth, pair of glasses, or lipstick look on me? Uncertainty is high and customers have a difficult time making the right decision. Given that customers can't "try" the product online, a personal visit to the store was often required to complete the mental image and see the "real" thing.

AR offers virtual showrooms, 3D displays, and holography through which customers can see exactly what they buy. They can see it 360 degrees, how it works, and how to operate it. Customers can also easily compare between options by putting them side-by-side or even sharing with friends to get their opinion. By bringing the physical world into the smart phone or tablet, AR boosts customer confidence that they can make the right decision. This reduces uncertainty to a minimum and makes it easier for the customer to serve themselves.

Educating customers — When customers serve themselves, they might have questions they need answers for. How do I replace this light in my car? What does a certain button on the portal does? Where are the foodstands in this park? Instead of seeking humans for help, customers can use AR. They can point their smartphones at the car light and get instant explanation on how to replace it. They can point their smartphone to the park map and get 3D directions to every foodstand.

AR is a unique hands-on training tool in explaining things. It adds an extra experiential element to the training process by offering interactive and immersive 3D presentations. Customers, even elderly ones, can more readily contextualize what they are learning by actually seeing what they have to do rather than reading or listening to lengthy instructions. The customer doesn't have to guess anymore. They do exactly what they see in the AR.

By simulating scenarios in a 3D version, the company can teach customers almost anything in a simple and easy way. The easier customers can learn, the more they can do themselves, making self-service more attractive. AR extends customer capabilities in understanding things and taking actions they could have never taken. It turns the layman customer into an expert technician that can install electronic devices and even fix problems that occur in appliances.

AR also helps in guiding customers through the self-service portal. AR shows the customer all the steps and actions that will be required once the option was selected. The customer can virtually press each button and see what happens next and know if that is the right choice, eliminating any sense of anxiety or concern in using the portal.

Consequently, using AR-powered self-service transforms the customer journey into a connected and immersive visual interactive experience. The positive outcomes extend to the company by reducing human contact volume, technician visits, and no-fault-product returns. Companies are on the ground floor when it comes to using AR. There is a lot of room for improvement.

A Great Example — Lowe's

The company built a virtual reality Holoroom How To. Customers go into a special room, put on the 3D goggles, and learn basic Do-It-Yourself (DIY) skills like tile a shower.

This is a great try-before-you-buy model, vastly improving customers' confidence in taking on DIY projects, willingness to try out new products, and making any decision they have to make on the way.

This VR tool has shown that it can improve unskilled customers' performance level comparable to that of experienced DIYers.

Conclusion

An effective autonomous self-service experience makes everyone happy. For customers, self-service is becoming first-service because they prefer serving themselves. It eliminates queues and waiting time to receive service from humans. Customers can decide when and where to get the desired service. For service providers, self-service reduces their need to deal with boring, mundane, and tedious issues. It motivates them to deal with the more complex issues. For companies, self-service makes them more efficient, helps optimize operations, and boosts the bottom line.

The tremendous benefits of self-service is the reason companies should cooperate with this trend and invest in it. Using AI and AR to reinforce it. Providing an appealing, easy to use, enjoyable autonomous portal that helps customers get what they need and enjoy a great experience.

References

[1] Zendesk (2013). Self-Service: Do Customers Want to Help Themselves? Available at https://www.zendesk.com/resources/searching-for-self-service/

[2] Furniss, B. (2014). 4 Steps to Enhancing Your Self-Service Strategy. Available at https://www.icmi.com/resources/2014/4-steps-to-enhancing-your-self-service-strategy

[3] Kulbyte, T. (2021). The Value of Customer Self-Service in the Digital Age. Available at https://www.superoffice.com/blog/customer-self-service/

[4] Shaham, H. (2018). AI Self-Service: Applications, Benefits & Best Practices. Available at https://techsee.me/blog/customer-self-service-artificial-intelligence/

[5] Commbox (2019). Customer Self Service: The Best-Kept Secret to Customer Satisfaction. Available at https://www.commbox.io/customer-self-service-the-best-kept-secret-to-customer-satisfaction/

[6] Kulbyte, T. (2021). The Value of Customer Self-Service in the Digital Age. Available at https://www.superoffice.com/blog/customer-self-service/

[7] Imre, P. (2022). Using Conversational AI to Improve Customer Experience. Available at https://medium.com/voiceui/using-conversational-ai-to-improve-customer-experience-1c7c9f8d1772

[8] Trout, M. (2017). Lowe's: VR, the Future of Retail. Available at https://digital.hbs.edu/platform-digit/submission/lowes-vr-the-future-of-retail/

[9] Mort, A. (2019). New Data Reveals How Critical Customer Service KPIs are Enhanced by Visual Assistance Technology. Available at https://techsee.me/blog/customer-service-kpis/

[10] Mital, A. (2018). Modernizing the Field Service Operations Industry with Augmented/Virtual Reality. Available at https://www.liveworx.com/blog/modernizing-the-field-service-operations-industry-with-augmented-virtual-reality

Lecture 11

Human Xperience:
People Serving People

"You can dream, create, design, and build the most wonderful place in the world, but it requires people to make the dream a reality."

Walt Disney

The seismic transformation that technology has made in the way service is managed and delivered raises a far-reaching question: Is the service provided by humans expendable? In other words, can technology provide as good of a service as humans and replace them? A few years ago the answer would have been: "Definitely no." But technology is advancing in such a rapid pace that now, in more and more cases, it can imitate a human and be an adequate alternative in certain situations. Currently, many customers who call companies receive service from machines (AI bots) and don't even know it.

While technology can be a good alternative in certain situations, it still can't simulate and replace employees' kindness, creativity, and the ability to think. It can't deal with complex, sensitive human problems or build authentic, personal connection and relationships. It can't be enthusiastic, supportive, and understand body language. The reason is simple. Technology is built to take care of the issues that customers raise as efficiently as possible. It's task-focused and efficiency-oriented. No small talk or gestures.

As technology becomes an even bigger part of our lives, and customer-facing employees become scarce, customers' desire for human-xperience won't disappear. In fact, the scarcer it becomes, the more it will be in demand. That is true today and in 10 or 20 years. But customers don't want just humans. They want engaged, courteous, and professional service providers that create value. They have no problem paying extra for it.

An Interesting Fact

Human interaction matters now.

About 82% of US customers and 74% of non-US customers will want more of it in the future.

A good 59% of all customers feel companies have lost touch with the human element of customer experience [1].

The way human-xperience is delivered is evolving with customers' changing needs. Historically, human service has been delivered through two main channels: Face-to-face and phone. These two channels have lost their appeal over the last few years because of the extra effort and inconvenience involved in using them. Physically coming to a place or calling, going through an automated telephone system, and waiting in queue to talk to a human is undesirable for customers.

New ways to make it easy and convenient for customers to talk to service providers are needed — valuable ways in which companies can bring human service to customers wherever they are, instead of customers coming to the company. That is, not a physical meeting of face-to-face but a remote one. This lecture provides an in-depth look at the different ways companies have to deliver remote human-Xperience.

The Value of Remote Human Xperience

Customers want human interaction, especially when they feel anxious and in distress. They want someone to accompany them and provide emotional support. Anything else won't suffice. What happens when such a situation occurs after business hours, or the customer can't physically come to the company or talk on the phone? Frustration mounts. At these critical moments, giving customers human interaction that they expect and need is priceless. Remote human interaction offers tremendous value to customers in several ways (Figure 11.1).

Anywhere the customer is — In today's world, with smart devices and advanced communication infrastructure, customers can receive remote human interaction whether they are at home, work, traveling, commuting, and even in the restroom.

Anytime the customer wants it — Remote access is slowly eliminating operating hours. The ability to work from home allows service providers to deliver service in the evening and even late at night. The company saves tremendous cost in office space and operations. Those savings can be used to compensate employees for delivering service at odd hours of the day.

Access to experts — Experts are a scarce resource in companies. How can the company make them available to all of its customers?

Figure 11.1. The Value of Remote Human Xperience

By centralizing resources. In the past, there was an expert at a specific branch or call center to deal with complicated customer issues. If nobody came to the branch, the expert's valuable time was wasted. The expert couldn't help another branch in which there might have been high demand for their expertise.

By remote access, every customer can easily access the company's most skilled experts. When a customer has a complicated issue, he or she is automatically routed to the experts and talks to them through the remote channels. The customer reaches the expert directly instead of going through the escalation route which is cumbersome, time consuming, and frustrating.

Amazon offers its customers a live support called Mayday. Press the Mayday button and get instantly connected via video to a tech expert advisor. The user sees the advisor live while the advisor only sees what's on the screen of the device. This combines quick help and privacy.

Instant human help — Remote service saves customers' time. When customers call a company, they might have to wait in a queue to be answered. It wastes their time and they don't always know how long it will take. When customers schedule a meeting with a service provider in a branch and a delay occurs, they have to wait and waste their time. In remote service if there is a delay, the service provider sends a message to notify the customer about the delay. The customer gets the message and continues with their work until it's time for the delayed encounter, avoiding wasting precious time.

Complete service data — In remote service channels, every detail of every conversation with each customer is recorded and saved on the company's systems. Every request, every question, every issue, and every action that occurred during the interaction. There is no need for service providers to manually document the conversation which is tedious and can be inaccurate or incomplete. The data can help people learn from mistakes that were made and to fend off unlawful lawsuits from customers.

The Five Channels of Remote Human Xperience

There are five major channels that can be used to deliver remote human-xperience:

1. Interactive text.
2. Live Video.
3. Virtual Agent.
4. Augmented Reality-enhanced human.
5. A Forum.

Each channel above is important and can yield exceptional experience when executed correctly. Customers should be able to choose the channel that best fits their liking, circumstances, and the issue they need to deal with. Let's take a closer look at each of the five channels to understand their unique characteristics.

Channel 1: Interactive text-xperience

Customers want and expect the company to make it easy for them to reach out and communicate when they need help. Several decades ago, it was the 1–800 free number that revolutionized the way customers receive service. Calling the company for free instead of physically going into it made this channel very popular. Even today, providing service through the phone is a powerful way to deal with customers. However, with high demand that leads to lengthy waiting and the addition of unfriendly automated system, calling has become less and less desirable.

In the last few years, the smartphone has revolutionized again the way customers want to be served. It made texting with service providers the preferred channel, with more than half of customers picking it over other channels [1].

An Interesting Fact

On companies' websites, 70% of customers chose a "message us" button over a "call us" button [2].

Social media interactions have made chatting and texting popular. One of the least used functions of the smartphone is the phone. Part of it is generational. Anyone older than 40 grew up talking to customer service on the phone. Anyone younger than 20 grew up messaging to interact with other people. But probably the main reason for the change is that texting is much quicker, easier, and more convenient than talking.

Customers can send a text under almost any circumstance — in places that talking is an issue (bar, concert) or not allowed (meeting, theater) at home, on a vacation, with friends, and while multitasking. That means service can be received under any condition without disturbing other people. Making service through texting a ubiquitous experience. If a call is needed, customers have to find a place where they can speak privately. Sometimes they can be on hold and ready for the service provider to reply, not being able to do anything in the meantime, and the call might be disconnected.

An Interesting Fact

Customers enjoy texting more than calling and the numbers show it. Customer satisfaction rates are 25% higher for chatting and messaging than for calling [3].

From the company's perspective, texting is also favorable. In phone support, one service provider can take care of one customer. In texting, one service provider can effectively handle multiple text conversations at once and thus serve multiple customers, reducing the cost to serve.

Delivering service through the phone has become a lose-lose situation for both customers and companies. Yet, billions of calls are made every year to call centers at a cost of over a Trillion dollar [4]. Despite this prevalence of texting, only 39% of companies have adapted to their customers' behavior and preferences in this regard [5]. That doesn't make sense. A change in emphasis, from voice to text, is needed if companies want to keep up with customer expectations and provide better experiences.

Texting can improve the customer experience in several ways (Figure 11.2):

Privacy — Texting provides customers with confidence that other people can't "hear" the information they are providing. Providing customers with high degree of confidentiality.

Clarity — When things are written down, less things are lost in translation, especially in conveying technical information or dealing with people who have accents.

Richer communication — The customer has an array of options to get the information across on texting platforms — Photos, videos, documents, and emojis.

Sharing — Customers can send information received from the company to friends and get their instant opinion.

Flexibility — Text allows customers to engage whenever they need to, without having to stay on a vigil for a support agent's response. The service can be stopped for a while and continued from the same exact point, allowing the customer and the company to respond when ready to.

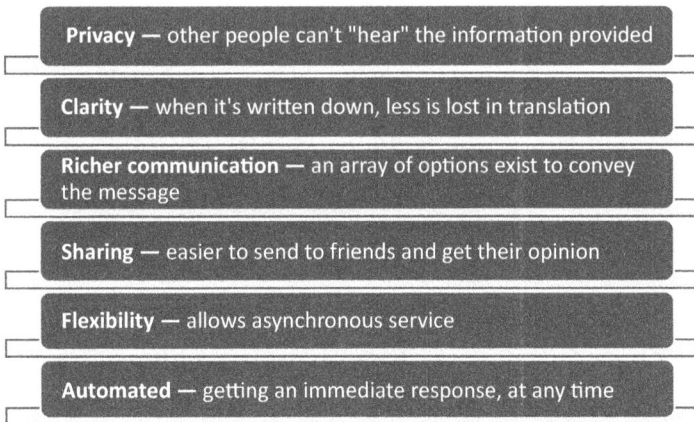

Privacy — other people can't "hear" the information provided

Clarity — when it's written down, less is lost in translation

Richer communication — an array of options exist to convey the message

Sharing — easier to send to friends and get their opinion

Flexibility — allows asynchronous service

Automated — getting an immediate response, at any time

Figure 11.2.   The Benefits of Serving Customers Through Texting

Automated — Customers text their issue and the company's AI recognizes the issue (Business hours, WIFI password, etc.) and instantly sends the customer a standardized written resolution. If more information is needed, the interaction can turn into a text conversation between the customer and the AI until a solution is reached.

Text messaging is a very effective way to communicate with customers. There is less friction and more speed. Done correctly, text can be as personalized and empathetic as voice. Writing the customer's name, using empathetic and caring words, and even using emojis. Consequently, with a simple text message, the customer can get things taken care off in real-time with little to no effort. That is an exceptional experience.

Channel 2: Live video-xperience

If a picture is worth more than a thousand words, how much is a video worth? With the improvement in the quality of mobile networks, video has become a trendy way to communicate between people. So why not use video as a legitimate channel to provide service? Companies have a real opportunity to leverage an increasingly popular channel to deliver a better customer experience.

Live video is the only channel that allows customers to enjoy a real face-to-face interaction remotely. That is a major advantage.

An interesting Fact
Customers' satisfaction rises by 50% when they use live video experience as compared to other remote human channels.

Live video uniqueness has several advantages that can improve the customer experience:

Eliminating mistakes — Live video allows better mutual understanding. The customer can show the service provider exactly what they need or what is wrong without the need to provide lengthy explanations or articulate the need using the right terms. The service provider can visually analyze the situation and guide the customer through the steps needed for solving the issue. They can watch the customer, making sure they are doing things right and stopping them before making a mistake. That increases first call resolution (an important method discussed in Lecture 12) [7].

Body language — Video adds a non-verbal dimension to the communication. The service provider gets a glimpse of the customer's facial expressions, gestures, and body movement that may indicate misunderstanding or dissatisfaction. These cues provide real-time insights into customers' emotions, allowing the service provider to be more empathetic. For example, a service provider issuing instructions for checking the cable connection can see confusion registering on a customer's face, enabling them to repeat or simplify the steps.

Diffuse tension — By seeing the service provider, tension can be negated as the customer knows they are talking with a real person and not a disconnected voice or a chatbot.

Video isn't just about live service. It's an effective tool in transferring information to customers and even teaching them. Experts in the company can record a video explaining to customers exactly what they need to do in different situations and showing them how to do it. The seeing part makes it much easier for customers to follow and be successful in doing things right. The videos can be placed on the company's website, self-service portals, and even sent to customers via email or social media channels. This ensures that many customers can watch, learn, and thus get the desired solution.

Channel 3: Virtual agent-xperience

A virtual agent (VA), also referred to as virtual assistant or chatbot, is a sophisticated software that can provide service to customers. With deep neural networks and natural language understanding, a

VA can imitate a human service provider. A VA can understand the needs and issues of the customer, hold dynamic conversations, and seamlessly interact with them to provide the necessary solution. Gartner found that 20% of all customer interactions happen through a Virtual Agent in 2022 [8], a figure that will only continue to rise.

Implementing VA platform in the company is an excellent way to optimize existing processes, provide fast and reliable responses at a lower cost, improve productivity, and extend the company's resources. A VA has no learning curve. There is no need for experience, no need for a lengthy and costly hiring process, extensive training, providing rewards and bonuses, or even making a work schedule. However, it's important to remember that when situations that require crafty actions or a human touch occur, just like in self-driving cars, a VA will ask humans to take over.

VA improves the customer experience by enabling the following benefits:

24/7 human-like availability — A virtual agent is always awake, day or night, ready to respond and provide immediate service.

A personalized experience — A VA knows the full history of every customer in the company. Once the customer calls, the VA automatically identifies the customer and draws important insights from the company's vast wealth of information. Using this data, the VA can offer responses and recommendations tailored to each individual customer with whom they're interacting. It adapts to real-time data, selection, and request to generate more accurate and effective responses to customer inquiries. For example, when a veteran customer calls, the VA will operate according to past history, utilizing things the customer likes while avoiding things they dislike. When a customer calls for the first time, the VA changes the tone, avoids jargon and provides longer, more in-depth explanations, taking the customer step-by-step at their own pace.

Shortened average handling time — In seconds, the VA receives the customer's request, goes through the customer's history as well as the company's data with regard to handling such an issue, and presents the customer with the best possible solution. There is no wasted time for reading the material or talking to the agent who dealt with the customer previously. Even if the customer has to be passed to a live agent for further actions, it's more likely for the average handling time is shorter. The VA has already handled part of the request and shows the live agent what was done and what issue is still left open.

Consistent performance — Every virtual agent provides customers with the same level of service every time, anytime, day-in and day-out. A virtual agent never gets tired, annoyed, or frustrated. There is no workplace drama. No attitude. Always providing the same information and the same complete answer every time the same question is asked. This creates consistency while reducing customers' uncertainty and helplessness.

Ensure compliance — VAs are constrained to a set of preprogrammed rules, therefore it's easy to ensure that every interaction is compliant with the relevant industry regulations and the company's rules. VAs keep up with every rule and compliance change. It can be constantly updated and seamlessly implements the change right away. Errors and misunderstanding rarely happen, which dramatically reduces failure.

Prevent problems — A VA doesn't just deal with issues that customers raise but also with issues the customer might not be aware off. While talking to the customer, the VA scans the account, databases, and billing history to see if there are any open affairs that need to be handled. Is there a late payment or maybe a subscription renewal due in a week? The VA deals with those issues and saves the customer the need to call again, wait in line, as well as deal with the negative outcomes that stem from not closing loose ends.

Handle demand effectively — Demand in service can fluctuate dramatically and quickly. The company has a limited number of human service providers. So when demands outpace supply, customers have to wait. VA solves that problem. Companies can have as many VA as they want at any time, with limited additional cost. When the volume of inquiries is enlarged, more VAs come online and have infinitely scalable abilities to deal with customers. When demand decreases, VAs go offline. Simple, straightforward, no problem. Customer call abandonment is reduced to a minimum especially at peak demand.

With dramatic advancements in technology, VA is going to be more and more like a human and less like a robot or a machine. Furthermore, VA is probably going to be able to understand customers' emotions from the sound of their voice and words they use. Consequently, VA advancement will lead to higher customer retention and renewal rates, increased sales conversion rates, faster resolution times, and higher customer satisfaction.

Channel 4: Augmented reality-enhanced human-xperience

Lecture 10 explained what Augmented Reality (AR) is — immersive 3D visuals that overlay images onto physical objects and environment via mobile devices. That lecture showed how AR provides customers with an interactive digital experience that dramatically improves self-service. Here, the focus is on how AR can enhance service providers in delivering remote human-xperience.

Remote customer support — Service providers can use AR to guide customers in real time assistance and solutions as if they're standing right next to them. Through AR and smartphone, the service provider and the customer see the same things and operate in tandem to solve the issue at hand (fixing internet connectivity), assemble a new product (installing a smoke detector), or do periodical maintenance (clean a copy machine).

Through AR, the service provider can literally show the customer what to do step-by-step (by circling or drawing on the screen) instead of explaining and verbally guiding them. A visual demonstration of action enables the customer to comprehend and execute the instructions faster than auditory communication. Especially with technical issues when the customer is usually not technical savvy. This hand-in-hand assistance is an effective way to get the job done right the first time, and do it quickly with limited hassle. Creating an experiential experience.

An Interesting Fact

By using VR, Vodaphone achieved the following results [9]:

- *10% increase in NPS and customer satisfaction.*
- *26% fewer technician visits.*
- *Enhanced employee experience. Service providers enjoy a more productive and natural way to communicate with their customers and are able to solve a wide variety of issues.*

Field services technicians — Assigning work orders in which the technician with the right skills get the right call is a daily challenge. If mismanaged, it can lead to increased costs and lesser productivity with more time being spent on the road and repeating visits instead of serving additional customers. AR is a great solution for this issue. AR allows any technician who is in the field to deal with any issue, even issues they never encountered or are too complicated for their skillset. In the past, such a situation requires another visit to be scheduled with a senior technician, wasting the customer's time and causing frustration. With AR, the field technician can transfer a live picture or 3D video of the situation at hand to a senior technician or a supervisor sitting at headquarters. They see what the field technician sees, analyze the situation, and guide the technician on how to solve the issue. Done right. No mistakes or additional visits. It's a simpler, easier, and cheaper way to provide great experience and satisfy customers.

AR also puts all necessary data and instructions in technicians' hands prior to dispatch. They can get familiar with the customer profile, history of problems, and a survey of the location for any potential access problems. This enables them to plan repairs before arriving on site and take special tools that might be needed, reducing wasted resources to a minimum.

The steady progress toward deeper implementation of AR into the service infrastructure is what the future has in store, providing higher and higher value to customers.

An Interesting Fact

Artificial Intelligence allows companies to [10]:

- *Boost productivity.*
- *Shorten repair time.*
- *Reduce the number of errors.*
- *Avoid common mistakes.*
- *Cut training time.*

Channel 5: Forum-xperience

Simply put, a forum is an online community in which customers interact with other customers. Customers enter a forum, engage in dialog with other customers, and talk to them about a variety of issues and topics. They learn from other customers how to fix a problem, deal with a complicated matter at hand, or avoid making a mistake. That is a unique remote human service in which the service is delivered by customers rather than service providers.

The forum isn't a new concept, but one that companies often hesitate to implement themselves on the company's website. The hesitation stems from the possibility of giving customers a public platform they might use to negatively talk about the company, its products, and services. While problems will surface, a forum is about finding solutions and people helping each other rather than trying to shame the company. Thus, it's more positive than negative. It gives veteran customers a voice they can use to help other people by sharing their experience. Veteran customers feel they are contributing which is also positive. Prospective and new customers are thrilled to get suggestions from experienced customers who use the product or service they just bought or are about to buy, increasing their chances of success.

The company can use its forum as well as other forums that customers use to get an in-depth insight into the customer experience. This enables the company to know what customers are feeling, struggling with, and what can be improved. The company shouldn't intervene in the discussion or defend itself in the face of criticism. It should only monitor the forum to prevent mistakes from happening. Customers who offer their knowledge, even experienced ones, can make mistakes, causing potential harm to other customers. By monitoring what is said, the company can intervene to stop mistakes from occurring or fix a mistake that was already done.

A forum improves customer experience in several ways:

Eliminates hassle — A forum eliminates the need to go through rigorous service scripts or a checklist of questions that service providers ask. They can sometimes eliminate an escalation of the issue to a manager. Instead, the question or problem is raised in the forum and other customers who encountered similar issues provide an answer or a solution with no hassle at all. Furthermore, customers feel more comfortable talking to a fellow customer especially when they can say "I have experienced this as well, and here's how I fixed it."

Wisdom of the crowd — Everybody knows more than any one expert. The forum has many people who used the company's products and services. Together, they probably know everything there is to know about the ins and outs of every product and service. The collective knowledge and experience make the forum unique in its abilities to provide answers to questions, solution to problems, and smarter, more efficient ways to use the product or service.

A sense of belonging — Human beings are social creatures who want to feel a sense of belonging. A forum offers customers exactly that — being part of a group, a community that helps each other. The cooperation between people develops a culture of connection in which people feel needed and wanted. It can also create friendships and business ventures between customers.

Frees up service provider's time — Allowing customers to be supported by other customers frees up time for service providers. The time saved can be used to handle complicated issues that the forum is unable to help with as well as serve customers who are unwilling or feel uncomfortable using the forum.

Trustworthy — Customers trust the opinion of a group of other customers they might not even know. The trust in them might be higher than the trust in the company. For example, when a customer sees that 486 customers gave a certain establishment a rating of 9.2 out of 10, they believe that place is excellent and will confidently stay in it. There is a reason that rating websites have a dramatic influence on customer behavior before they try a place, product, or service.

In a forum, customers share thoughts and exchange ideas about missing features in products or services. They share wishful thoughts about options they would love to see. This is a great starting point in driving innovation and coming up with the next big opportunity (see Figure 11.3 on the next page).

A forum has benefits inside the benefits. The more customers use the forum, the more knowledge is shared. The more questions and answers are collected and the more problems and solutions are

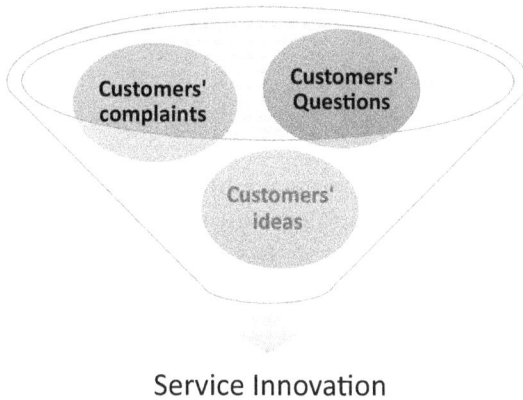

Service Innovation

Figure 11.3.   What Leads to Service Innovation

dealt with, a more comprehensive collective knowledge entity emerges. The company can capitalize on this knowledge and use it to improve many aspects of its operations. Also, the company can learn from the unique perspective of customers — how they think, and how they use uncommon, out of the box solutions.

Conclusion

People use more and more technology. But when a stressful or anxious moment occurs, people want to talk to humans. That is human nature and it's not going to change. However, the channel to get human service is changing. Moving from less convenient channels of face-to-face and phone to simpler and easier channels, discussed in this lecture, that offer remote human experiences.

By offering customers easy access to humans through remote channels, both sides are happy. Customers get what they want by talking to real people and not Bots, or doing things autonomously. The company enjoys flexibility in handling customer demand and providing a human-xperience at a lower cost. That is a winning formula.

References

[1] Puthiyamadam, T. and Reyes, J. (2018). Experience is Everything: Here's How to Get it Right. Available at https://www.pwc.com/us/en/services/consulting/library/consumer-intelligence-series/future-of-customer-experience.html

[2] Fowler, G.A. (2018). Want Better Customer Service? Don't Call. Text. Available at https://www.washingtonpost.com/technology/2018/08/09/want-better-customer-service-dont-call-text/

[3] *Ibid*

[4] IBM, (2022). AI Chatbot That's Easy to Use. Available at https://www.ibm.com/blogs/watson/2017/10/how-chatbots-reduce-customer-service-costs-by-30-percent/.

[5] Telus International, Customer Service Channels, (2019). Best Practices for Superior Customer Service Through Text Message. Available at https://www.telusinternational.com/articles/best-practices-customer-service-text

[6] Simonneau, D. (2019). Three Measurable Benefits of Video-Enabling Your Contact Center. Available at https://blog.vidyo.com/customer-engagement/video-contact-center/.

[7] *Ibid*

[8] Imre, P. (2020). Using Conversational AI to Improve Customer Experience. Available at https://medium.com/voiceui/using-conversational-ai-to-improve-customer-experience-1c7c9f8d1772

[9] Shaham, H. (2018). Global Innovator Vodafone Partners With Techsee for AR Remote Assistance. Available at https://techsee.me/blog/vodafone-innovation-augmented-reality/

[10] Shaham, H. (2018). Augmented Reality in Customer Service: A Success Story. Available at https://techsee.me/blog/augmented-reality-customer-service/

Part 4

Develop and Enhance the Xperience

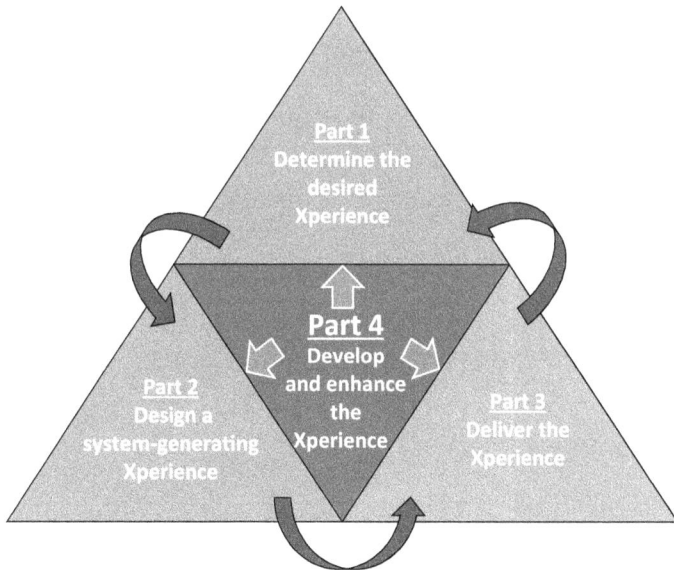

The 4D Xperience Model

Delivering an experience is a never-ending journey. It starts when the customer first contacts the organization and ends when they leave for good. In between, every time the customer makes contact, a positive experience has to be provided all over again.

In today's experience economy, the bar for satisfactory service level keeps being raised. Customers of companies with exceptional service have become accustomed to simplified and seamless transactions and a high degree of accessibility, reliability, and personalization. This gets them to expect and even demand similar levels of service from other companies.

Providing a great experience has many positive outcomes. Delivering the same experience consistently time after time preserves those outcomes. Nevertheless, with disruptive competition coming from all directions, a favorable experience might quickly become less favorable if the competition offers more.

To keep up with customers and competition, companies have to raise their standards. The experience provided has to evolve, adapt, and improve. Preserving the competitive advantage while keeping customers happy, willing to spend money, and recommend the company to others.

To advance and strengthen the experience, the company has to track, measure and analyze the encounters with customers and constantly enhance them. It also has to follow future trends to make sure the experience of tomorrow is reshaped to meet customers' upcoming needs.

Lectures 12, 13, and 14 help understand how to assess, scrutinize, and figure out successfully the quality of the experience that organizations provide as well as ways to improve it.

Lecture 12

Xperience Measurement Program

"Whatever the measurement system is, it needs to be consistent, repeatable, and as unbiased as possible."

Pearl Zhu

Peter Drucker once said, "What gets measured, gets done." It goes even further. What gets measured is important, can be managed effectively, and can be improved. An effective customer experience measurement program is a key factor in consistently delivering a great experience. It tracks, collects, and measures the customer experience three-hundred-and-sixty degrees from the first encounter till the customer churn. It checks expectations, feelings, and perceptions of the service provided. Once that information is assembled, actionable insights can be extracted to effectively revamp the organizational system, develop people's skills, and upgrade the customer experience.

A successful customer experience measurement program helps the company know what is done well and what has failed, understand important patterns of behaviors, and identify opportunities to delight. Seeing whether people are up-to-par with the company's service standards and cater to customer needs. It allows the company to take the right initiatives that will help it stay relevant and ahead of market trends.

Simply put, measuring means listening outside to customers, and inside to managers and employees. It's hearing everything they have to say (comments, suggestions, questions, etc.), what they like, dislike, and what they expect to get and actually got. When customers and employees are heard loud and clear and are treated accordingly, a beautiful synergy occurs in which everyone gains.

Measuring the customer experience takes a big part of the guesswork out of managing customers. Decisions are based more on facts and data than gut feelings or assumptions. Getting things right more often than not. Using customer data to operate and manage the company enhances the customer-oriented strategy and experience.

A well-designed measurement program requires substantial resources, dedication, and persistence. That is an expensive investment worth taking. Done correctly, a successful program is imperative in generating business growth and improving profitability.

A successful experience measurement program has several distinct characteristics and metrics, but it starts with collecting the proper data.

An Interesting Fact

The measurement of customer experience in most companies has four major flaws [1]:

1. *Limited — only 7% of the customer voice is shared.*
2. *Reactive — only 13% are confident that their organization can deal with CX issues in near real time.*
3. *Ambiguous — only 16% think the measurement system allows them to address the root causes of poor performance.*
4. *Unforced — only 4% think the measurement system enables them to calculate a decision's return on investment.*

Collecting Experience Data

Measuring means collecting data. To measure customer experience, data on customers has to be gathered. There are various methods companies can use to collect data. Those methods can be categorized into direct and indirect.

Direct methods ask customers straightforward feedback about their experience. These more invasive methods require customers to spend time providing the required information. With many busy customers skeptical of questions or uncomfortable with providing information, direct methods can cause inconvenience and lead to a relatively low response rate.

Indirect methods gauge the customer experience without directly involving them. In these less intrusive methods, the company monitors interactions with customers and observes their behaviors and actions instead of asking them directly. These methods measure almost all customers, but there is a limitation of how in-depth the data will be.

An Interesting Fact
Only 32% of customer experience professionals feel they have access to the information they need to understand customer's needs and previous interactions, and can apply it to improve their experience [2].

Here are short explanations for techniques in each method.

Examples of direct methods techniques

Surveys — Probably the most common way to ask customers for information. There are many types of surveys; they vary in length, format, and purpose. A survey involves a questionnaire that asks customers about their thoughts and feelings from their interactions with the company. The survey can be given to customers at three different times: During the service encounter, following its conclusion, or at any time the company wants to learn something from customers. The questionnaire can be handed physically, done over the phone, through SMS, App, email, and any other form of communication. Surveys can be placed on the company's website, Facebook wall, or anywhere else the customer interacts with the company. That gives customers the opportunity, whenever they choose, to speak up and let the company know what they think.

Customers' focus group discussion — This involves a group of people who are gathered to discuss prepared topics regarding their service experience with the company. These groups can include existing or potential customers. The topics can range widely, allowing the company to get in-depth perspective and get the necessary information they need from the group. The company can better understand what customers think, feel, like, dislike, agree or disagree with, etc.

In-depth interview with customer — This is an intensive, in-depth talk conducted with an individual customer. The goal is to explore deeper, more emotional insights and perspectives they have about the experience or the company. This lets the company discover behaviors, usage barriers, and reveal emotions that would be impossible to find using other techniques.

Feedback kiosks — These are terminals with a set of buttons — from a smiley face to a sad face, from green to red, that can be physical or virtual in which the customer can press or click the button that best represents their experience at the point of encounter. The terminal, which is easy to install in various strategic places, allows the company to get in-the-moment accurate feedback. These types of kiosks are highly noticeable, require no time, and thus invite customers to respond. As a result, response rates are usually higher than other forms of direct methods. However, there is no way to follow up with customers who press the button because it's anonymous. Furthermore, the feedback might be misleading when customers (especially children) press the buttons aimlessly.

Examples of indirect methods techniques

Online tracking — When customers interact with the company using internet-based channels (website, app, social media, etc.), every action, click, or swipe is tracked. What customers looked at, for how long, and what was the outcome, can be monitored. This allows the company to see traffic flow, understand content usage and interests as well as behavior patterns, habits, and possible actions and reactions. Companies can follow transactional data on each channel, enabling them to know the most and least popular channels. Then they can use the data to improve and enhance both.

Social media posts and comments can also be tracked. Those mentions offer genuine, non-filtered emotions and feelings. Customers say what they think with a high degree of candidness because they aren't talking to the company but to people like them. Hearing what customers ask, say, and suggest can offer important information and crucial data for measuring the experience that customers received.

An Interesting Fact

- *About 74% of customers get frustrated when they receive content, offers, ads, promotions, etc. that has nothing to do with their interests.*
- *At least 57% of people are OK with providing information on a website as long as it's for their benefit and is used in a responsible way.*
- *A good 77% of customers would trust companies more if they explained how they are using personal information to improve their online experience [3].*

Transcripts analysis — Live chat, e-mails, letters, and phone calls are documented or recorded. Reviewing those transcripts can provide important feedback on the customer's interaction with the company and overall experience. Frequently mentioned topics, commonly asked questions, and specific words used are information that can be gathered to learn more about customers and their experience.

Although qualitative transcripts can be cumbersome to review, they tend to offer employee-customer interaction insights that can't be achieved through other methods.

Front-line employees' discussions — Employees interact with customers and thus are excellent sensors to what is going on. They constantly see, hear, and observe what customers are doing. Their knowledge and understanding of service nuances is priceless — what works in the company and what doesn't, what customers want and don't want, what can enhance the experience and make customers happy, and what doesn't. Talking to employees isn't just about getting information, it's also about making them feel important and that they contribute to the company's success. This motivates them to implement changes that are based on their input.

Gathering data with direct and indirect methods on a daily basis from multiple channels is the first step. The next step is to understand the characteristics of an effective measurement program.

Characteristics of a Successful Experience Measurement Program

An effective measurement program is able to capture the experience from every aspect. Thus, providing the company with a complete picture of what happened in each encounter. Such a program usually includes the following characteristics.

Includes both the outcome and the journey — Every service encounter, whether physical or digital, ends up with an outcome — what the customer got out of the interaction. But there is another component that is equally important to measure — the customer journey. This is the entire process (touchpoints, interactions, etc.) that the customer goes through to get the outcome. The outcome and the journey together determine the experience.

Combines the rational with the emotional — Measuring what customers think (rational) about the experience is important. Measuring how customers feel (emotions) about the experience is equally important. Emotional reactions can influence rational decisions for some customers and vice versa for other customers.

Everyone is measured on the same metrics — When everyone in the company, from executives through the various management levels all the way to employees across departments are measured on the same experience metrics, they all aim toward achieving the same goals. They make sure the company's customer-first vision, strategy, and culture are implemented every day. At Lego, everyone's bonus, from the CEO to the customer service associates, is based on the NPS score (a customer loyalty metric discussed later on in this lecture) [4].

A Great example — John Lewis

John Lewis Company ensures that employee satisfaction and customer satisfaction are inextricably linked. All its 84,700 staff reaped an additional 17% bonus, which is worth nine weeks' pay — from the CEO to the man who washes dishes in the café because of better customer satisfaction results [4].

Mixing different time frames — Customer perception of the encounter can be different if someone asked them about it right after it ended or after a few hours or days. At the moment, the experience is fresh in their mind and can offer specific details about the encounter. After some time has passed, they can convey more in-depth thoughts and feelings about what happened. Both aspects are important.

An individual customer's experience isn't defined by a single interaction. It develops over multiple interactions. The measurement system has to follow each customer over time to see their accumulative experience. This provides an important perspective in understanding the health and the strength of the relationship the company has with its customers.

A simple feedback experience — Without customers' feedback, the measurement program is useless. Companies need relatively high customer response rate to get accurate data. Customers don't have to give feedback. The company needs their feedback. Making the feedback process easy and inviting increases the chances of customers responding to the request and providing the desired feedback.

Using multiple sources — To truly gain customer insight, multiple sources of data across the entire organization should be used. This means gathering information from the sales team, call center, operations, marketing, website, complaint management system, and others. The different data sources provide a much broader understanding of the customer's experience.

Having sound methodology — The data gathering and analysis has to be based on accurate, precise, and reliable procedure. Allowing a more accurate and successful analysis that result in bettering people's performance and the company's business results.

A successful measurement program is sound and clean of mishaps, inaccuracy, and confusion. Averting potential mistakes will ensure the program isn't compromised.

Common Missteps in Measuring Experiences

Companies invest heavily in customer experience measurement. Yet, many struggle to achieve effective results. Part of the struggle stems from mistakes that are done while performing the measurement. Being aware of these blunders will help avoid them, automatically improving the effectiveness of the measurement. Here is a list of missteps to avoid (see Figure 12.1 on the next page).

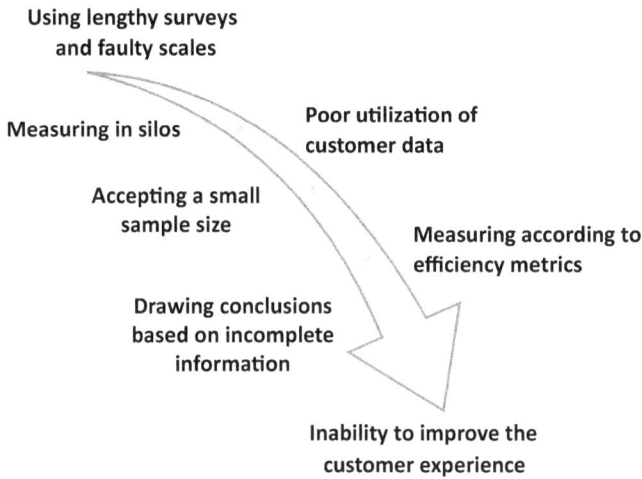

Figure 12.1. Missteps in Measuring Experiences

Using lengthy surveys and faulty scales — In an attempt to get as much data as possible on customers, companies put more and more questions into the survey, making it long and often cumbersome. A lengthy survey usually causes customers to avoid filling the survey given the effort involved. The shorter, the better. Fewer questions and minimizing time-to-answer makes the survey much more compelling to fill.

Measuring customer experience in a binary scale — "yes" and "no" or even a 1 to 5 scale don't provide enough variance to exhibit accurately the level of customer experience. Scales from 1 to 7 or 1 to 10 offer a wider range of options that customers can choose from. Resulting in a more exact rating.

Accepting a small sample size — A small sample size might not be a reliable and accurate representation of the broader customer base and the actual, truer customer experience. This is especially important if the company has diversified groups or categories of customers with unique characteristics. The same is true when measuring employees' service performance. Employees serve many customers every day. Measuring an employee on a specific encounter or even two or three encounters can provide a false representation of their abilities to deliver experiences. The employee might have provided a poor service in a specific encounter or two, but was excellent and provided great experiences in the rest of the encounters that were not measured.

Drawing conclusions based on incomplete information — Customers increase their usage of the company's self-service kiosks. Is that a positive or a negative outcome? Drawing a conclusion based on this data might not be that simple. The conclusion can be positive, if the kiosk lets customers do what they need quickly and they love it. However, the conclusion can also be negative if they are unwillingly forced to use the kiosk because the line of people in the branch is always long.

The number of complaints has decreased dramatically. Is that good news or bad news? Maybe the company improved the level of experience and decreased the number of errors made. Or maybe customers realized that it's not worth the time complaining because nothing comes out of it. Without additional information to help better validate the data, there is no way to know. Overall, drawing conclusions from any single data set might provide an incomplete picture and sometimes a misleading one.

A good way to avoid this mistake is to include two or three open-ended questions or even adding the word "Why?" on the survey. Such questions provide insights into what customers are thinking and the reasoning behind their rating. Making the data more complete and the conclusions that follow, more accurate.

Poor utilization of customer data — Companies collect a vast amount of data on customers. Unfortunately, the data usually is saved on computers, the cloud, and even in cabinet files and not analyzed or used on a daily basis. As a result, opportunities to personalize the service and enhance the customer experience are lost. Even worse, customers often have to repeat information that the company already has, deteriorating the quality of experience and their perception of the company.

Measuring according to efficiency metrics — Efficiency metrics such as average handling time, total number of customers handled per day and hold time, may lead to higher productivity, but often hurt the customer experience. With efficiency metrics, it's within the employee's self-interest to keep calls short, transfer hard-to-solve problems to another team, and sidestep complicated or challenging problems. All of these lessen the customer experience. Average handling time doesn't allow the opportunity to build long-term relationships with customers or take the extra mile.

Measuring in silos — When each department measures its own service performance, measuring the entire customer experience is often forgotten. That may lead to conflicting results. Customers may be satisfied with every single department, but unhappy with the experience as a whole. That is, customers were served well at each touchpoint but were frustrated and unhappy that they had to go through several touchpoints instead of just one.

Experience Metrics

There are numerous metrics used to measure customer experience. The question is: How many metrics and which metrics should an effective measurement program include?

Too many metrics makes the measurement system cumbersome and too complex to understand. People have a difficult time following all the metrics. On the other extreme, encompassing only two or three metrics might be simpler; but no matter how good the metrics chosen, they provide only a limited perspective of the customer experience. This hinders the ability to understand its quality and consequences in a deep and meaningful way.

The old adage says: "Measure what matters." Matters to whom? Simply put, it's about selecting the metrics that capture the

Figure 12.2. The Benefits of Getting the Experience Metrics Right

customer experience in a way that helps the company continuously improve it (Figure 12.2). Making customers happier and the company more successful. A win-win situation.

Whether physically or digitally, the measurement program has to assess the two components that make up the customer experience — the journey (the process of dealing with the issue at hand), and the outcome (the resolution or nonresolution to the issue). Let's take an in-depth look at essential metrics that can be used to measure accurately each of the two components.

Customer Journey Metrics

Getting a resolution to a request requires customers to go through a journey in which they interact with employees or technology, state their request, take certain actions, provide information, and even perform tasks. This journey can be placed on a scale. At one end, the journey is simple, effortless, short, and flawless which results in delighting customers. On the other end, the journey can be complicated, unfriendly, long, and cumbersome which results in frustrated customers. There are four major metrics that can tell any company where on the continuum it stands. All four should be measured to provide a holistic view of the journey.

Metric 1 — FTR — First Time Right. This answers the question: Are customer requests dealt with in the right manner the first time, from start to finish, every time?

Metric 2 — TTR — Time To Resolution. This answers the question: How fast do customers get their issues resolved?

Metric 3 — CES — Customer Effort Score. This answers the question: Do customers have a difficult time getting the service they need from the company?

Metric 4 — SBC — Service By Channel. This answers the question: Are customer requests dealt with in the most efficient and effective channel?

FTR — First time right

FTR (in call centers it's often referred to as FCR — First Call Right) measures the percentage of customer contacts (whether face-to-face, phone, or online) that were resolved in one interaction out of all customer contacts the company had in a certain time frame. Customers dislike repeating, retaking, or redoing things. They want everything done right the first time, every time. They want to get all the information, understand what has to be done, and provide an accurate resolution that fits the customer needs and expectations in one encounter.

With today's technology, it's relatively simple to follow customers and see how many times they contacted the company to deal with the same issue or if they started online and ended talking to a live person suggesting the resolution wasn't found online.

The higher the FTR percentage, the more customers are satisfied with the encounter. The higher the FTR, the lower the cost-to-serve customers is for the company. Making it more cost-efficient.

TTR — Time to resolution

TTR measures the length of time it takes to resolve a customer issue from the moment they made contact with the company on any channel to the moment a suitable solution was offered and accepted by the customer. A long or short resolution time isn't a binary result — positive or negative. Long can be negative if customers waited time in vain for no reason. Long can also be positive if the customer had the time to ask questions, got the attention they needed, and resolved the issue with no loose ends. The same can be said with short resolution time. Short is positive if the customer got what they wanted quickly. Short can be negative if they were rushed and didn't have time to ask questions. Usually, the shorter the time to resolution, the lower the cost is for the company as shown in Figure 12.3.

TIME TO RESOLUTION	APPROXIMATE RESOLUTION COST
IMMEDIATELY	$4.70
WITHIN 24 HOURS	$4.70
2-3 DAYS	$7.80
4-7 DAYS	$7.80
1-2 WEEKS	$15.70
3-4 WEEKS	$15.70
OVER 1 MONTH	$23.50
STILL UNRESOLVED	$23.50

Figure 12.3.　The Effect of Time-To-Resolution on Cost

Source: https://www.zendesk.com/blog/retailers-customer-service-imperatives/

TTR is about getting the customer in and out as quickly as possible without rushing them or making them feel they are on-a-clock. Being efficient to save them time, rather than being efficient to increase productivity and handle more customers. In other words, moving at the pace of the customer. If the customer wants a prompt, in-and-out response then fast is the way to go while preserving accuracy and quality. But if the customer wants more time to understand the options and weigh each one, then long TTR can still result in a satisfying experience.

CES — Customer effort score

CES measures how much effort a customer exerts to get what they need from a company. Effort can be physical, psychological, or emotional. A flawless, simple, and smooth encounter requires no effort. Friction points, complexity, confusion, and other hurdles along the way require customers to put forth extra effort. It can be finding desired information both physically or online, going through rigorous processes, repeating information, and even as simple as the need to click too many times to move the process along.

CES is measured by asking a single question: On a scale of 1 to 5, how much effort was required from you to get a specific issue or request resolved by company X? The statement will depend on the interaction they just completed. The five-point scale ranging from 1 — "Very Easy" (effortless journey) to 5 — "Very Difficult" (excessive effort journey) is an inverse scale in which the lower the CES score, the better the customer journey experience.

SBC — Service by channel

SBC measures the percentage of contacts that used the right channel to deal with their specific request. Customers contact companies for different reasons — questions, problems, issues, comments, ideas, etc. They use a variety of channels (chat, phone, Facebook, etc.) Every channel has advantages and shortcomings. Thus, every channel is suited to handle certain requests more efficiently and more effectively than other channels.

The company has to follow the different reasons why customers make contact. Then, check to see how efficient each request was handled in each chosen channel. Over time, the company can see which channel is the best fit to deal with each request. This enables the company to provide sound recommendations for customers on which is the ideal channel to choose regarding the request they have. Customers don't have to comply with the suggestion and can continue to use the same channel. But if they try and see that the proposed channel is more efficient, the probability of them switching and staying with the new channel are high. A win-win situation occurs. Trust is built. The next time the company offers a different channel for them to try, they will probably listen and benefit from it.

Customer Outcome Metrics

At the end of the service journey, customers receive an outcome. That outcome can be satisfactory or not. It determines their actions, whether it's to stay with the company, leave, criticize, recommend, or take other actions. These actions are important because they determine the company's success and financial performance. There are five major metrics to measure customer reaction from the outcome.

Metric 1 — CSAT — Customer Satisfaction. This answers the question: Are customers pleased with what they got?

Metric 2 — RFM — Recency, Frequency, Monetary. This answers the question: Are customers signaling that they are about to leave?

Metric 3 — NPS — Net Promoter Score. This answers the question: Would customers recommend the company?

Metric 4 — NSA — Next Step Action. This answers the question: What are customers going to do next?

Metric 5 — LTV — Life Time Value. This answers the question: What is each customer's long-term worth?

CSAT — Customer satisfaction score

CSAT measures how much customers enjoy interacting with a company. It's probably the most simple, intuitive metric a company can use. CSAT is measured with one overarching question "How would you rate your overall satisfaction with the service received from the company?" Customers rate this question on a 7 or 10 point scale that on one end is "extremely satisfied" and the other end is "extremely unsatisfied".

The general question can be broken down into several specific questions that focus on certain touchpoints or aspects of the experience. CSAT can measure satisfaction immediately after the encounter, a few days later, or any time the company chooses to know where it stands with customers.

It's important to remember that "satisfaction" is subjective and means different things to different people. Two customers receiving similar service to the same request at the same time frame may have totally different satisfaction scores due to situational and personality factors.

RFM — Recency, frequency, monetary

RFM measures the probability that customers are about to churn. The metrics is based on three data points:

Recency — When was the last time the customer contacted the company?

Frequency — How often does the customer purchase at a set time frame?

Monetary — How much does the customer spend at that set time frame?

Each of these data points provides important information about the customer and possible intentions. Recency — a customer who visited the company once a week and hasn't for a while may indicate they are going somewhere else. Frequency — a customer who visited twice a week for the past year and now visits only once a week may indicate they are going somewhere else. Monetary — a customer who spent a certain amount per week for the last year and reduced that amount substantially may indicate that they spent the rest of the money somewhere else.

According to the metric, when all three indicators occur together (hasn't visited in a while, reduced the number of visits, and spent less), a red flag is raised. It indicates a high probability that the customer is planning on leaving or is already on the way out. This provides a heads-up notice, giving the company an opportunity to be proactive and contact the customer to fix the situation.

NPS — Net promoter score

NPS measures customer loyalty to a specific company. NPS is based on asking customers one close-ended question: "On a scale of 1 to 10, how likely are you to recommend company X to a friend or colleague?" It's recommended to add "Why" at the end of the question, asking customers to explain why they gave the score they did. This allows the company to better understand what went right and pinpoint failure areas.

NPS scale is divided into three categories: Customers who give a score from one to six are referred to as detractors, those who give seven or eight are referred to as neutrals, and those who give nine or ten are referred to as promoters. Only promoters are considered loyal. NPS is measured by subtracting the percentage of promoters from the percentage of detractors. The score can range from plus 100% to minus 100%. The higher the NPS, the better the experience and the company's financial performance.

NPS can be moved from the macro level (overall NPS for the organization) to the micro level using the question to measure individual products or services, individual stores, web pages, or even staff members.

There is an important issue to remember when it comes to NPS. While companies measure it, customers constantly provide NPS online (through any site that has rating.) After receiving the experience, some customers respond online by giving "a score", "stars", "likes and dislikes", and "positive comments". These are in essence, NPS results. A five-star rating or a like, are promoters. Low rating, negative comments, and three stars or less are detractors.

Companies should be aware of their online NPS scores because prospective and existing customers are. Their actions are determined by those scores. This data is real, straightforward, and without filters. It offers a bare truth statement of the company's experience. The company can also get the "why" from online rating. Customers share their thoughts on why they gave the rating. Listening to customers on forums, communities and groups will provide a detailed explanation on why they gave the grade they did.

A Good Example — Apple

Apple conducted an interesting research on NPS. Managers at the company stores called customers who gave an NPS score of six or less (detractors). Then they tracked those customers' purchase patterns against customers who were also detractors but didn't get a call from the company. The findings showed that contacting the customers resulted in an additional spending of more than $1000 over time. Together, all the customers who were contacted increased revenues by $25 million in the first year [5].

A Good Example — Philips Electronics

Philips Electronics tracked NPS scores and found that where the scores increased, revenue grew by 69%, where scores remained steady, revenue grew by 6%, and where scores declined, revenues actually decreased by 24% [5].

NSA — Next step action

NSA measures what customers are going to do after every encounter with the company (NPS focused on one of those actions — recommending the company). NSA is also based on asking customers a single question: "Following your latest encounter, what will most likely be your next step?"

While other measures looked at what happened, this measure focuses on understanding what will happen. This allows companies to prepare for what is coming and redesign the experience accordingly, strengthening areas that led to positive outcomes and desirable actions and preventing mistakes and unwarranted actions.

Unlike other metrics, this metric doesn't have a scale, only a list of possible actions, for example:

• Ask for help.
• Buy Less.
• Get an offer from competitors.
• Look again at the product on the company's website.
• Read about the importance of the service in review sites.
• Use live chat instead of calling.

The possible answers can change according to the industry or a specific touchpoint. The number of answers shouldn't exceed seven or eight, to avoid respondent fatigue. A good option is to include an "Other actions, please specify." That can help customers who feel that none of the options exactly convey their answer. It also provides companies with ideas for potential next steps they didn't think about.

CLV — Customer lifetime value

CLV measures how valuable a customer is to the company over time and not on a transaction-by-transaction basis. It's well known that keeping existing customers costs less than it does acquiring new ones [5]. Repeat customers usually spend more and often recommend the company. These are positive outcomes any company would welcome.

CLV is unique because it's tangibly linked to revenue and profit from customers rather than intangible outcomes such as satisfaction and loyalty. CLV is calculated in the following way:

$$\text{CLV} = \begin{bmatrix} \text{Customer} \\ \text{revenue} \\ \text{per year} \end{bmatrix} \times \begin{matrix} \text{Duration of the} \\ \text{relationship in} \\ \text{years} \end{matrix} \quad (-) \begin{matrix} \text{Total costs associated} \\ \text{with acquiring and serving} \\ \text{each customer individually} \end{matrix}$$

This calculation shows which customers are worth more and which customers are worth less and are even unprofitable. If the cost to serve an existing customer increases dramatically, the customer may turn unprofitable despite the high revenue they might generate. Calculating CLV over time enables the company to rank its customers by importance and take actions accordingly. Thus, improving the effectiveness of those actions.

The Financial Impact of Experience Metrics

The metrics discussed above measure effectively the customer experience and correlate with the company's financial performance. Companies that achieve better rating on experience metrics have higher profitability than companies that falter on these metrics. Specifically, the metrics correlate with revenue growth and lower overall costs. Here are a few examples:

Higher revenue growth:

- There is a positive correlation between revenue expansion and the level of NPS. Companies at the upper quartile of NPS scores see a 24% growth in revenue while those at the lower quartile see only a 9% growth [6].

- A staggering 94% of customers reporting low CES said they would repurchase, and 88% said they would even increase their spending [7].
- For every 1% improvement the company makes in FTR, it gets a 1% improvement in customer satisfaction and thus have repeat customers and repeat purchases. On average, customer satisfaction drops by 15% every time a customer has to call back about the same issue [8].

Lower overall costs:

- Improving FTR would save the average call center almost $400,000 annually [9].
- Low CES interaction costs 37% less than high CES interaction [10].
- About 65% of respondents decided to return non-defective electronics products citing high CES factors such as frustration or confusion during product unboxing, installation, and initial usage [11].
- When TTR is immediate it costs the company approximately $5. When TTR is two or three days, the cost rises by more than 50% to $7.80. A delay to one week will double that cost even further [12].

Measuring Employee Experience

As mentioned in previous lectures, internal service is correlated with the external service. Similarly, there is irrefutable evidence linking employees' experience to customer experience [13]. Thus, measuring the employee experience can provide a good indication of whether employees are happy, engaged, and dedicated to serving customers and helping the company achieve its goals.

Given the employee-customer experience correlation, the metrics used to measure the customer experience (NPS, CES, CSAT and FTR) can be used, with minor changes, to measure employee experience.

E-NPS — Employee net promoter score

This metric measures employees' loyalty to the company. The same question from NPS is used with minor changes: "On a scale of one to ten, how likely are you to recommend friends or colleagues to work for the company you work for?" The scale is divided the same — promoters, detractors, neutrals. The calculation of the overall score and the range is the same (from +100% to –100%). High E-NPS means most employees like the company and promote it. A low score means more disengaged employees and lower performance.

E-CES — Employee customer effort score

This metric measures how difficult it is for employees to perform their job efficiently. The same question from CES is asked with minor changes: "On a scale of 1 to 5, how difficult is it for you to perform daily tasks and deliver the desired customer experience?" Lower score means the system makes it easy for employees to do their job, while a high score means the system hinders employees from doing their job and delivering quality service.

The more effort employees have to put forth to deliver an experience because of complex and unfriendly processes, bureaucracy and lack of empowerment, the less motivated they are to do it. They see no reason to exert the extra effort. In contrast, when things run smoothly, employees have more energy to invest in serving customers.

E-SAT — Employee satisfaction score

This metric measures how satisfied employees are at their job. It uses the same question but changes the narrative "How would you rate your overall satisfaction from the company as an employee?" The general question can be broken down into several specific questions that focus on certain aspects of the job and the working environment.

E-FTR — Employee first time right

This metric measures the quality of the company's internal service. Specifically, it measures how many of employees' requests from the company, other departments, or their manager were resolved in a single interaction from A to Z. With no need to repeat, retake or remind people to do what they were asked or supposed to do. Employees, like customers, want everything done right the first time, every time. It makes work life easier.

Together, these metrics are a great indicator of employees' level of engagement, loyalty, and performance. Allowing the company to find out what impedes employees and develop better strategies for managing their experience at work.

Conclusion

An effective measurement program helps manage the experience more as a science than an art. It constantly monitors the system, tracks service progress, and follows customers' journey and outcome using the information to hold people accountable. It makes sure everyone is aligned with the company's service standards and business objectives, pinpointing what isn't working well so that the right changes are made to enhance experiences for both customers and employees.

References

[1] McKinsey & Company (2021). Prediction: The Future of CX. Available at https://www.mckinsey.com/business-functions/marketing-and-sales/our-insights/prediction-the-future-of-cx

[2] Lumoa, (2022). The Ultimate List of 100+ Customer Experience Statistics for 2019. Available at https://lumoa.me/customer-experience-stats

[3] Enaohwo, O.M. (2022). How Online Personalization Can Create Compelling Customer Experiences and Build a Better Business. Available at https://neilpatel.com/blog/online-personalization/

[4] Scott, A. (2022). How Silos Damage Customer Experience. Available at https://www.matchboard.com.au/how-silos-damage-customer-experience/

[5] Lumoa, (2022). The Ultimate List of 100+ Customer Experience Statistics for 2019. Available at https://lumoa.me/customer-experience-stats

[6] Zimmer, C. (2018). Does a Better Net Promoter Score (NPS) Result in Better Business Performance? Available at https://glympse.com/blogs/does-a-better-net-promoter-score-nps-result-in-better-business-performance/

[7] Campbell, P. (2018). NPS Revenue Correlation: Impact of NPS on Revenue Expansion. Available at https://www.profitwell.com/blog/nps-retention-benchmarks

[8] Levi, D. (2022). Customer Effort Score (CES): Your Complete Guide to Earning One. Available at https://techsee.me/blog/good-customer-effort-score/#:~:text=According%20to%20the%20HBR%20study,of%20those%20experiencing%20high%20effort

[9] ITSM, (2022). Ready for ITSM at High Velocity? Available at https://www.atlassian.com/itsm/service-request-management/first-call-resolution

[10] Geraghty, S. (2014). Why You Should Measure First Call Resolution. Available at https://www.talkdesk.com/blog/why-you-should-measure-first-call-resolution/

[11] Gartner, (2019). What's Your Customer Effort Score? Available at https://www.gartner.com/smarterwithgartner/unveiling-the-new-and-improved-customer-effort-score/#:~:text=Low%2Deffort%20interactions%20result%20in,and%2054%25%20of%20channel%20switching

[12] Mort, A. (2019). 2019 Consumer Electronics Survey: NFF Returns. Available at https://techsee.me/blog/nff-survey/#:~:text=2019%20Survey%3A%20NFF%20Returns&text=The%20survey%20demonstrates%20that%2041,and%2Dmortar%20and%20online%20retailers

[13] Kramer, S. (2018). 10 Stats Linking Employee Experience with Customer Experience. Available at https://fowmedia.com/stats-linking-employee-experience-to-customer-experience/#:~:text=That's%20simple%E2%80%94customer%20experience%20is,record%20of%20poor%20customer%20experience

Lecture 13

Intelligent Customer Analytics

"We see our customers as invited guests to a party, and we are the hosts. It's our job every day to make every important aspect of the customer experience a little bit better."

Jeff Bezos

The owners of a Mom & Pop's neighborhood grocery store knew each and every customer personally. They knew their history inside and out, their specific needs and expectations. They knew who wanted what, when, and how. Every Friday they saved a loaf of bread for Miss Carmicle, a newspaper copy for Mr. Menendez, and told Miss Freeman that someone will bring her the groceries knowing she was under the weather.

The little grocery store provided such a wonderful experience that it grew over the years and turned into a grocery chain with thousands of customers. The owners could no longer remember the profile of every customer and keep track of their needs. Going through the existing massive database was no longer humanly possible. To keep the level of experience high and make the right decisions, a new method was needed.

Along came a tool called customer analytics (a definition is offered later on). By employing this tool, the grocery chain was able to process the vast amount of data collected and perform deep analysis to continue and provide a personalized experience to each and every customer. The objective was to find positive outcomes and enhance them; uncover pain-points and fix them; understand customer behavior patterns, be proactive, and surprise them. Consequently, to help a giant grocery chain to continue and provide a Mom & Pop's neighborhood store-like wonderful experience.

Using customer analytics might sound simple. It's not. There is a need to collect quality data and use sophisticated statistical methods to analyze the data. The analysis findings have to generate actionable insights and useful information that is shared across the company and injected into the decision-making process and everyday actions from top to bottom. People have to embrace the findings and constantly use them.

These aren't easy tasks to perform. But they are doable when people understand how an effective customer analytics program looks like. This lecture outlines the components of such a program.

Customer Analytics Overview

Customer analytics is a mandatory tool in delivering great customer experiences and improving them. This tool enables companies to track customers and learn everything about them. Then, use that information to manage the company, make the right changes, invest resources effectively, and determine how people should interact with customers. Eliminating much of the guesswork and ensuring better, more accurate results and less mishaps. Here are a few basic questions and answers to better understand customer analytics.

What is customer analytics?

Customer analytics, sometimes referred to as behavioral analytics, is a process of studying customer data to learn how customers behave and act, understand habits they follow, and the way they make decisions. An effective process furnishes companies with fact-based information and insights that help choose the best course of action in every situation. It also helps manage customers effectively, improve the organizational operation system, provide a better value proposition, enhance relationships, and ultimately optimize the experience.

Why is customer analytics important?

Customers are more empowered and connected than ever. They have access to information, they do their research, and want companies to give them something extra and better. Customers know the company is collecting data on them and they expect the company to use that data to treat them accordingly while offering solutions that fit their situations and preferences. Companies have to meet and exceed customers' expectations and analytics is the best tool to help them do just that, making it not "nice to have", but a necessity.

Customer analytics uncovers both golden opportunities to delight customers, and shortcomings to fix broken promises. It figures out what customers are missing, looking for, or asking about. It finds ways to make processes more effective and efficient. It empowers people to execute their job to the best of their abilities and make better decisions. It creates a valuable offering by delivering a more accurate interaction that attracts and retains customers rather than alienate them. This enables the company to increase customer loyalty and financial results (see Figure 13.1 on the next page).

What are the benefits of customer analytics?

Companies that effectively utilize customer analytics achieve tremendous outperformance because of four major reasons:

Retaining customers — Customer analytics can identify common denominators among lost customers even when the metrics might not show it. It gives an early warning that existing customers may be in danger of churn, allowing the company to take corrective actions, fix the situation, and retain those customers. This helps keep existing revenue and positive cash flow.

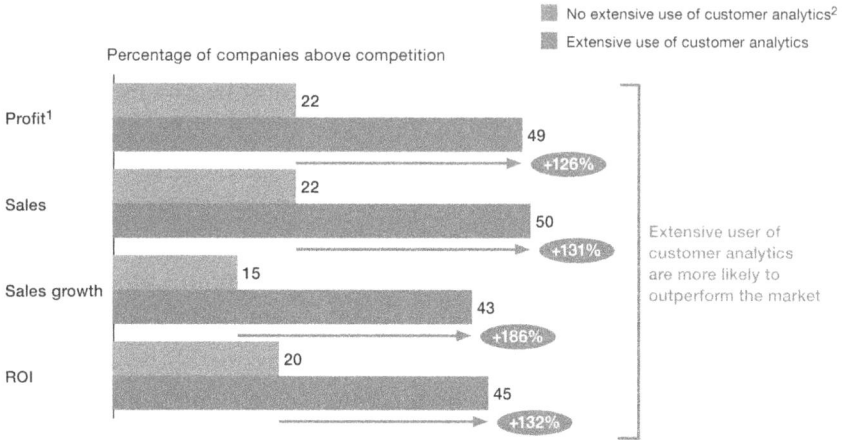

Figure 13.1.   Customer Analytics and Companies' Performance

Source: https://www.mckinsey.com/business-functions/marketing-and-sales/our-insights/five-facts-how-customer-analytics-boosts-corporate-performance

Revenue growth — Customer analytics can identify loyal customers' purchasing decisions as well as the buying processes and factors that have both a positive and a negative impact on these factors. It helps the company find ways to reduce sales cycle time, improve conversion rates, and find the best opportunities to cross-sell and up-sell, all of which improve revenue growth.

Reduced costs — Customer analytics can identify pockets of inefficiency and ineffectiveness drainers (futile processes, unproductive actions, and recurring mistakes) that lead to wasted resources, increased costs, and frustrated people. This helps the company focus its improvement efforts on areas that result in substantial savings of money and resources.

Improved profit margins — Not all customers are created equal. Some customers are more profitable than others. Some customers are unprofitable and the company loses money by keeping them. Customer analytics gives concrete insights into each customer, allowing the company to change its investments accordingly and thus get more out of each investment. Analytics can also build a profile of the company's best customers. Give that profile to sales people so they can focus on attracting those value-added customers. Significantly reducing the cost associated with attracting unprofitable customers.

An Interesting Fact

Companies that utilize customer analytics are 126% more likely to be ahead of the market in profits, 132% on return on investment, and almost twenty-fold higher on customer profitability [1].

The Customer Analytics Process

Customer analytics is a never-ending process. The process never stops because customers never stop. There are always new needs and new issues that have to be addressed. The data continually flows. While the process is endless, it can be broken down into three recurring steps:

Step 1: Customer Data Collection — Creating a comprehensive and accurate customer data base.

Step 2: Data Analysis — Extracting useful information and actionable customer insight from the data.

Step 3: Data driven actions — Using the analysis findings to enhance the customer experience and improve the organizational system.

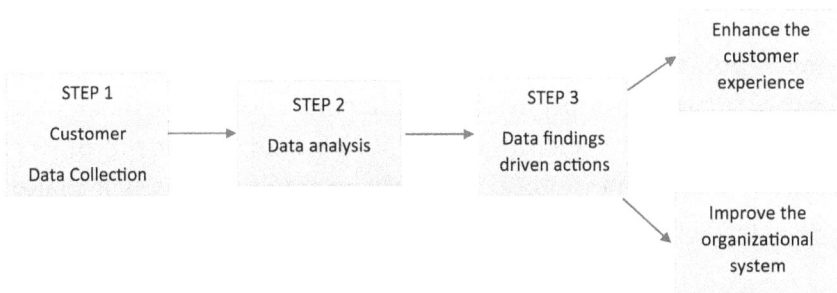

Before the three steps are outlined, here is a demonstration of how the three-step process happens in companies.

Step 1 — A hospital collects data on each patient. From personal profile and medical history at the first visit, to medical procedures (X-rays, CT scans, and MRIs) and follow-up visits along the treatment.

Step 2 — All the information is analyzed by the physician using AI and machine learning tools to decide on the best possible treatment. The diagnosis involves analyzing other patients with similar medical problems treated in the hospital in the past or in other hospitals around the world. The analysis might show that putting people with similar treatment in the same room saves time and reduces mistakes. Consequently, people and technology ensure that the best possible course of action is chosen every step of the way.

Step 3 — Doctors, nurses, and other staff follow the treatment to a tee. Customer analytics monitors the patient and helps doctors see how the treatment is progressing. Everything is done on-time the right way and thus reduces mistakes to a minimum. Patients are effectively treated and the organization operates efficiently.

Let's understand the three steps by taking a more in-depth look at each one.

Step 1: Customer data collection

Data collection is a meticulous, costly, time-consuming process. But it's a mandatory one for delivering experience. Data is a vital resource for the company's success. Without data, customer analytics is pointless. Data isn't enough. The data has to be accurate, thorough, and comprehensive. Inaccurate or superficial data drive faulty and unreliable results which leads to missed opportunities, poor experiences, and lost customers. This is a major concern for many companies. A study found that at least 60% of retailers either don't have detailed, solid data or have unreliable data. The average company's data is only 55% accurate and more than 14 months old, which renders the data essentially useless [2].

In life, every time we meet someone, the first thing we do is collect data. We ask "How are you? What is new? How is the family? Kids? Job?" and many other questions. The more information we obtain, the better we can learn and connect. The same is true for companies. When it comes to customers, collecting data is the only way to really get to know what they want, their limitations, preferences, etc. The more data there is, the better the analysis will be, improving the chances of delivering a great experience.

Data collection has to be at the top of the to-do list. Constantly gather customer data from every encounter, channel, and source. Every piece of information is important even if that information isn't relevant at that particular moment. When customers contact the company, employees often focus on the issue at hand, while ignoring important information the customer might share on other issues and life events. That information might not be currently relevant, but valuable for future interactions. For example, while the employee takes care of the customer's issue, the customer says his ten-year old son has an important basketball match in half an hour so he needs things to move along quickly. That information about the son is irrelevant in fixing the mistake that occurred in his account. Yet, it's extremely valuable when the employee asks the customer about the son's match before the next interaction starts. That builds rapport and strengthens loyalty.

Data comes from two main places:

1. **Externally** — Any source outside the company (customers, suppliers, competitors, publications, etc.)
2. **Internally** — Any source within the company (employees, managers, executives, data analysis, etc.)

Data collected from the different sources ensures a well-rounded understanding of the experience that the company provides. The data collected can be classified into five distinct types (Figure 13.2):

Descriptive data — Provides a personal profile of each and every customer. That information includes, a general description, identity, family details, lifestyle, career, preferences and more.

Transactional data — Describes what exactly happened during the service encounter. That can involve everything from a question the customer asked to internal processes that were used, to employee actions and consequently customer reactions.

Usage data — Deals with how customers handle and operate the product or service they purchased. From unboxing the product or the first time they used the service, to what they think about its continuous usage, through the quality of support in answering questions and solving problems. All the way to buying the next product/service.

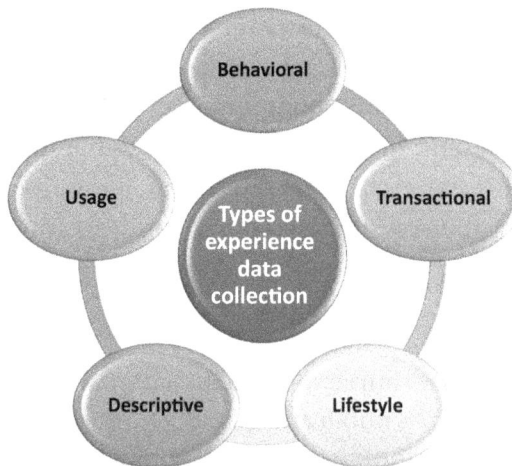

Figure 13.2.   Five Types of Data Collection

Behavior data — Includes every action the customer makes while interacting with the company online. From website views, clicks and browsing, to engagement behavior (questions, reviews, comments, and posts), self-service preferences, chat usage, etc.

Lifestyle data — Covers the way customers live and the daily choices they make. The information comes from new technology sources such as smart devices, in-home automated machines, App, and wearables. Collected data can be customers' habits, fitness routines, health indicators, and much more.

When collecting data, there is a major obstacle that many companies face and have to overcome. That obstacle is data silos — a situation in which one team or one department gathers certain data on customers that other teams or departments can't get access to. These silos often result from:

- Unwillingness to share information or knowledge because of competition or animosity.
- Highly departmentalized organizational structure in which each department is focused on itself rather than cooperating with other departments.
- Different technological systems and numerous databases across different functions that lead data to be stored in multiple places. This makes it challenging for many to access specific data.

Data silos leads to wasted resources in which multiple teams work hard to collect and store the same data. It also hurts the customer analytics effectiveness because the access to some of the information is denied.

Asking the right questions

A great way to collect meaningful data is to ask relevant questions. There are countless questions to ask. Questions that drive the customer experience should be in focus. Superb questions are clear, concise, can be proved or disproved, and tie back to the company's core service strategy and customer-centric objectives. Subjective or relative questions like "Is our service the best?" are difficult to clearly answer and thus are of lesser quality.

Here are ten questions that companies would be happy to get answers for:

1. What does an optimal customer experience look like?
2. What is the profile of the most profitable customers?
3. Where in the customer journey does churn happen and why?
4. What improves the interactions between departments?
5. What service provider actions correlate with high customer loyalty rates and positive word-of-mouth?
6. What are the customer issues that service providers have the most difficult time resolving?
7. Why do some customers use the reward program or loyalty card constantly while others don't?
8. Why are customers returning a specific product?
9. What causes customers to physically come to the store to complain instead of using online options?
10. Which touchpoint creates the most customer dissatisfaction?

Data collection is essential. Yet, no matter how good and comprehensive the data collected is, it's irrelevant if the next step in the customer analytics process — data analysis — isn't done correctly so it can produce meaningful insights from the data.

Step 2: Data analysis

Data analysis is the process of mining the company's database to discover useful information and valuable insights that are hidden in mind-numbing rows of numbers. In other words, it's looking at what happened in the past, interpreting, and learning from it in order to make better decisions, take more accurate actions, and avoid service blunders in the future. Allowing the company to optimize the customer experience and maximize results.

Data analysis is nothing new. Since the early 20th century, companies have been applying "scientific" management techniques to get better outcomes from their assets. Over the last decade, with breakthroughs in technology, modern sources of data and new statistical methods, algorithms and software platforms, and data analysis findings are much more meticulous and comprehensive. They help companies connect the dots, discover relationships and correlations, identify customer behavioral patterns, as well as uncover market trends, service gaps, and much more.

Types of data analysis

Data can be analyzed in several ways and deal with different aspects of the data. Here are five major types of data analysis:

Descriptive analysis — Answers the question "What is happening right now?" This analysis summarizes customer experience in real time. It provides real-time visualization of the company's operation through a dashboard. It shows if there are currently any problems with the service delivery. That could be lengthy wait time, high bounce rates on the company's website, spike in shipment delays, etc. It's usually the first analysis done and sets the foundation for other analyses.

Diagnostic analysis — Answers the question "Why did it happen?" This analysis drills down to uncover the reasoning behind certain outcomes and discover the root cause of the issue at hand. Such an analysis allows the company to move from dealing with problems to preventing them altogether.

Predictive analysis — Answers the question "What is likely to happen in the future?" This analysis uses historical data to make predictions about future outcomes. Predictions aren't facts. But when based on a detailed data-set and a comprehensive in-depth analysis, they are also not guesses. They are high probability estimations that happen often.

A Good Example — DiDi Chuxing

This Chinese ride-sharing firm uses its 450 million customers and 25 million rides each day to generate a predictive rating score for almost every ride. Those predictive scores match up very reliably — more than 80% and improving — with what customers say in traditional Net Promoter feedback [3].

The company can also predict with high certainty whether a customer is likely to return and spend more, churn, or become an advocate or detractor of the company. These predictions are critical in the way the company allocates budgets, invest resources, and manage the customer experience.

Prescriptive analysis — Answers the question "Which is the best course of action or response to take for each situation?" This analysis looks at the current situation with the issue, problem, or decision at hand. Then, it looks at similar scenarios in the past, what actions were taken, and which action was the most successful and led to the best possible results. According to the trial-and-error data, the analysis looks for a feasible solution to problems faced in the past and currently facing or could face in the future. This is a classic "Learn from the past" to "Do it better in the future."

Text analysis — Also known as text mining, answers the question "What are customers writing about the company?" This analysis involves classifying text responses, extracting connections, interpreting trends, and looking for similarities and patterns in texts from emails, chats, social media posts, reviews, and comments. For example, analyzing online reviews to understand customers' views, opinions, and sentiments towards the company by classifying each as positive, negative, or neutral. Also, understanding specifically what customers like and dislike about their experience.

An effective data analysis includes a combination of the types of analysis discussed above. Yes, it will take more time and resources to use several types of analysis, but the benefits greatly outweigh the cost.

A Good Example — Sephora

The successful cosmetic company uses the different types of data analysis.

Descriptive analysis — The company analyzes its customers' online shopping behavior, habits, favorite products, specific time they like to shop, profitability, and the like.

Diagnostic analysis — The company analyzes what causes some customers to purchase and others not to.

Predictive analysis — The company estimates how much additional purchases can be gained if it offers important information along the journey, provides help, discounts, and so on.

Prescriptive analysis — The company uses the analysis to find the best possible customer journey out of different service channels. The analysis recommends giving certain customers a freebie product will increase their future purchases.

Text analysis — The company looks at everything customers write to personalize future experience and improve its effectiveness.

To get context, Sephora analyzes its competitors to know where it stands with regard to its performance, products, and customer experience. Sephora was a disruptor company. Now as an established entity, it understands the importance of being aware of such rising competitors so it can prepare and constantly improve its service offering and value to customers.

Analysis outcomes

The analysis outcomes are aimed at improving the customer experience, boosting satisfaction, and loyalty. Done right, the data analysis produces two major outcomes: Useful information, and actionable experience insights. Let's further understand the two concepts.

Useful information

Useful information helps people in the company to know more about customers and better understand them. That information includes customer personalized data such as background, preferences, needs, habits, routines, as well as how profitable they are. Also, customer encounter history with the company which includes buying behavior, complaints, product return, special request etc. Finally, it includes answers to frequently asked questions by customers.

Useful information can be divided into two levels: Organization level and personal level.

Organizational level useful information — At this level, the information is aimed at helping executives and managers learn about areas of strength and uncover areas of weakness for improvement. It allows them to pinpoint where investment and changes should be made to get the highest return. Here are a few examples of such information:

- Knowing how many new customers came from each service channel and which channel had the highest conversion rate (turning visitors to buyers). Which specific touchpoint and actions lead to the conversion and how many of the buyers eventually became brand advocators.
- Showing which touchpoints cause customers extra effort that dissuaded them from continuing their purchase or terminating even their relationship with the company altogether.

- Displaying the reasons for which discounts are valuable to customers and which aren't.

A Good Example — Netflix

The company knows which series its customers are watching and for how long they continue watching it, or at what point they switch to something else. The analysis showed that a large number of customers started to watch a canceled series by binging on its previous seasons. This finding propelled Netflix into investing the necessary resources in producing another season of that series.

A Good Example — DiDi Chuxing

The company can instantly identify situations where there's some need for relationship or service recovery, triggering an intervention. If DiDi's algorithms identify a pickup that is going to go awry or a ride that took longer than it should have to reach the destination, the company can issue an apology or give the customer a refund before they even exit the vehicle [4].

A Good Example — Amazon

The company looks at every customer's purchase history, wish list, shopping cart, or preferences by items rating and profile. That useful information is used to pair people with similar interests and makes product recommendations. The reasoning behind the idea is that people often get the best recommendations from someone with comparable profile to themselves. This strategy generates approximately 35% of the company's annual sales [5].

Individual level useful information — At this level, the information is aimed at helping service providers be prepared, make smarter decisions, create a better, more fruitful interaction with customers, provide a compelling service, and avoid mistakes that waste resources. Here are a few examples of such information:

- The service provider receives information that a specific customer likes to be addressed only as Mr. or Dr. and not in any other way.
- The system shows the service provider that the next caller has complained twice in the past two weeks, the content of the complaints, and what was done.
- The service provider is notified that the wrong advertisement was sent to customers, many of them called, and wait time is high.

Having useful information on customers and knowing what to expect doesn't mean service providers will always know the best course of action to choose in every situation. There are often several options to choose from. How do they choose? Does each person make their own decision? The answer is no. Actionable experience insights derived from the data analysis help service providers take the right actions.

Actionable Experience Insights

Actionable experience insights aren't more information or more data. They are direct advice on which actions to take. When actionable insights are executed, they have meaningful positive impact on the organizational system, job execution, and service delivery. The more insights harvested and executed, the better the outcome.

Actionable experience insights can also be divided into two levels: Organizational level and personal level.

Organizational level actionable experience insights — At this level, experience insights provide executives and managers with fact-based actions that solve large-scale, organization-wide issues. Here are a few examples of such actionable insights:

Issue #1: There are high bounce rate in the product pages of the company's website.

The actionable insights: Tweak the product details, increase the number of product images, and add customer reviews of product usage.

Issue # 2: Returning customers are unhappy because they aren't eligible for the first-time discounts anymore.

The actionable insight: Encourage customers to sign up to the company's newsletter that offers them "returning customer discounts".

Issue # 3: Customers who enjoy the company's experience aren't providing recommendation.

The actionable insights: Call customers after a positive encounter and ask them to write a positive review and upload it onto the company's website. Or, call long-time loyal customers and ask for a short video recommending the company.

A Good Example — Canada Goose

The company's customers had a difficult time assessing how good a coat is in very low temperatures. They would try the coat on in the store, but since the temperature wasn't really cold, they couldn't know.

The actionable insight was to build a cold room instead of a dressing room. This allowed customers to test the coats in extreme low temperatures and experienced the coat under the "right" conditions and know if it provides the necessary solution. The cold room also helped customers understand how these low temperatures influence their bare face and overall body feeling from head to toe.

A Good Example — IKEA

The company observed people's behavior and saw that there are limited ways to charge smart devices at home and it's often uncomfortable. They also realized that furniture in the house had nothing to do with charging. After extensive research, an actionable experience insight arose — integrate charging into the furniture.

These insights led to the world's first line of furniture with integrated wireless charging capabilities, allowing customers to charge the devices by placing them on the furniture. Something that intertwined into their everyday life, habits, and routines. It became part of a successful initiative to bring smartness into homes and make it accessible to the mass consumer market.

Individual level actionable insights — At this level, actionable insights guide employees into taking the right actions, choosing the right options, and personalizing the interaction with each and every customer. They empower service providers to act quickly and be proactive, giving customers the best possible solutions to their issues. Here are a few examples of such actionable insights on the individual level:

Issue # 1: A customer called for a second time about the same problem.

The actionable insight: Service provider gets the best words and sentences to use in such a case, what kind of compensation to offer, and if to involve a manager or not.

Issue # 2: The customer didn't understand the service provider's explanation.

The actionable insight: Offer the customer a short video that explains this issue.

Issue # 3: Customers who started to use the chat option instead of the phone were satisfied with the change.

The actionable insight: Offer customers who called the company to try the chat option the next time they call.

Issue # 4: Customer made a mistake and asked for something that doesn't exist.

The actionable insight: Apologize for the misunderstanding and offer customers two other options that replace the erroneous advertisement.

In conclusion, data analysis can uncover the key positive and negative drivers of customer experience. Something no human can spot, no matter how smart or experienced they are. Those drivers are translated into useful information and actionable insights that provide opportunities to do things better. Data analysis minimizes trial-and-error format that leads to costly mistakes and lessening as much as possible the luck-factor.

As good as the data findings are, they are meaningless if not implemented in everything the company does and embraced and acted upon constantly by people performing their work. That is the third and final step in the customer analytics process.

Step 3: Data findings-driven actions

The data analysis findings have to be implemented to enhance the customer experience and improve the organizational system (operations, processes, and practices). The goal is to prescribe various workable, fact-based, and even proven remedies to effectively deal with customers in every situation and improve their experience. Choices, actions, and decisions backed by data analysis finding often lead to better results than just basing them on intuition, gut-feeling, hunches, or subjective perceptions.

An Interesting Fact

McKinsey Global Institute found that data-driven organizations are 23 times more likely to acquire customers, 6 times as likely to retain customers, and 19 times as likely to be profitable [6].

Data findings-driven actions lead to strong organizational results because they provide the following benefits:

Faster implementation — When everyone is working according to the analysis findings, there is no need to wait for managerial approval. Everything is straightforward. No runarounds or bureaucracy that slows things down.

Higher consistency — When everyone is basing their actions according to the analysis findings, they follow a similar path in comparable situations. This creates consistency in the level of service delivered across the company.

Continuous improvement — Data is constantly collected, updated, and analyzed. The new findings are implemented to fine-tune existing actions, enabling the company to continuously improve itself.

In the end, no one can force people to use the analysis findings (information and insights). It has to become an integral part of the organizational culture and second nature for people. Operationally, data findings lead to actions when the following conditions happen:

- **The right person** — Executive, manager, or employee.
- **Gets the right findings** — Different people from different departments get the information and insights that are relevant and applicable to their job and situation.
- **At the right time** — The moment the person needs it with no wait.
- **Anytime** — Accessible 24/7.
- **Anywhere they are** — At home, work, on the road, in the field, on their computer, cell phone, or tablet.
- **Accurate** — Up-to-date and completely reliable findings.
- **Coherent** — Presented in an easy and simple summary form, easily read and interpreted, convenient to browse through and find the necessary details.

When people from top to bottom get findings that enable them to accomplish their job better, they will continue and use those findings and trust the process. Executives use the data to make the organizational system more efficient and flawless. Managers and service providers use the findings to improve their overall performance and the company's level of customer experience.

When data findings-driven actions are adopted by everyone in the organization, customers are happy with getting higher value, managers are happy with better performance, and executives are happy with boosted financial results (Figure 13.3). This is a win-win-win environment.

As the digital world unfolds, customers are loyal to companies that make their lives convenient and get them what they need faster and easier than anyone. However, that loyalty once set in stone for years is now up in the air. The next company that comes along and makes customers' lives even more convenient, does things faster even if not cheaper, will get their attention and then their business. Without analytics, it will be next to impossible to consistently make things simpler, faster, and more convenient than the competition, placing the company's future in jeopardy.

Figure 13.3. The Benefits of Effective Analytics

Source: https://www.researchgate.net/figure/Reported-Benefits-of-Predictive-Analytics_fig7_325934828

The Three-Step Customer Analytics Process — Conclusion

Overall, the analytics process is a kind of a laboratory — gathering data and information (Step 1); performing in-depth analysis on the data (Step 2); searching for patterns, actionable insights, and other useful information; using those findings to improve operations and actions to create magical experiences (Step 3). Then, repeating the whole process again and again and again.

This endless loop of collecting, testing, uncovering, learning, tweaking, improving, and changing for the better is the way to consistently drive value that leads to customer engagement, loyalty, and success.

Future Trends in Customer Analytics

Customer analytics is transforming the way companies operate, manage people, and interact with customers. It's a transformation that is only going to intensify given the constant improvement in the field of analytics resulting from disruptive technologies, new algorithms, and advanced research methods. Understanding key trends that the future holds for analytics will help companies prepare and adjust for what's coming. Here are some trends to follow:

End-to-end, 360-degree analytics

An integrated, cross-departmental analytic process will be required. No more data silos, but a complete picture of the customer journey from A to Z. This end-to-end, integrated perspective provides deeper, more complete insights that can further the customer experience.

Casual inference

Finding out what leads to what, understanding what causes a particular customer to do X while another customer does Y — understanding the root cause of customer behavior can help the company have a better control on the desired outcome.

Artificial intelligence as a chief detective officer

AI analytics can and should monitor the company's every aspect, metric, and outcome. It should automatically send alerts when organizational standards are breached or goals aren't met. It doesn't end there. The AI will provide possible causes for the drop in a certain metric, including proof (just like a detective) and explanations for the reasoning behind the drop.

IoT (Internet of Things) analytics

With more and more smart devices and connected appliances, companies will have to analyze this connected environment. Figuring out how customers use products and what causes problems, frustrations, and delight in their daily life. Enabling the company to facilitate increasingly personalized service.

Data quality management

With massive amounts of data collected, companies are often overwhelmed and even paralyzed. They have a difficult time separating the insights from the noise. As a result, the company becomes data-rich but insight-poor. New analytical tools and methods will help change this situation by intelligently combing through the data and cherry-picking only high-quality data, eliminating error, noise, and reducing the wasted resources of poor data quality management [7].

Emotion analytics

Emotions influence customer actions and thus have a big role in determining experiences. Understanding the influence of those emotions on customers is becoming an increasingly important issue.

New tools such as visual recognition and natural language processing will help companies track, follow, and analyze customers' emotions. Allowing companies to manage those emotions, deal effectively with negative emotions when they occur, and prevent actions that lead to damaging emotions.

Customer analytics is shaping the way companies connect, transact, and engage with customers and create value. It guides the organization in the quest to become more agile, flexible, and preserve its competitive advantages. Embracing and implementing the trends above will help companies continue to strive and grow.

Conclusion

Customer analytics is a fundamental resource that every company has to adopt, implement and operate. It's the only tool that takes data, multiplies it exponentially, and turns it into useful intelligence that helps the company optimize its performance and get a leg up on competition.

Companies that don't fully embrace customer analytics will lose out on exceptional opportunities in delivering high quality experiences and improving financial results. Once the transformative power of analytics is understood, it is quickly embraced, and no one ever looks back.

References

[1] Fiedler, L, Perrey, J., and Pickersgill, A. (2014). Five Facts: How Customer Analytics Boosts Corporate Performance. Available at https://www.mckinsey.com/business-functions/marketing-and-sales/our-insights/five-facts-how-customer-analytics-boosts-corporate-performance
[2] Wolkow, R. (2022). What is Customer Analytics? Available at https://alp-stars.com/what-is-customer-analytics/

[3] Markey, R. and Springer, T. (2017). The Future of Feedback: Sometimes You Don't Have to Ask. Available at https://www.bain.com/insights/the-future-of-feedback-sometimes-you-dont-have-to-ask/

[4] *Ibid*

[5] Arsenault, M. (2022). The Amazon Recommendations Secret to Selling More Online. Available at http://rejoiner.com/resources/amazon-recommendations-secret-selling-online/

[6] Fiedler, L, Perrey, J., and Pickersgill, A. (2014). Five Facts: How Customer Analytics Boosts Corporate Performance. Available at https://www.mckinsey.com/business-functions/marketing-and-sales/our-insights/five-facts-how-customer-analytics-boosts-corporate-performance

[7] Anodot, (2022). The Price You Pay for Poor Data Quality. Available at https://www.anodot.com/blog/price-pay-poor-data-quality/

Lecture 14

The Future of
Customer Xperience Leadership

"The term 'customer experience' won't exist in the organization of the future. It will be so deeply entrenched in a company's product, process, and culture that it will be synonymous with the brand and represent the only way to do business."

Ann Lewnes, SVP and CMO, Adobe

The COVID-19 pandemic has reminded us that what is working great today might become inept tomorrow. It also reminded us that being customer-centric and delivering great experiences is a winning formula under any conditions. Customer-centric companies can quickly change and adapt to new customer needs, new situations, and new norms. The strong relationships built with customers enable those companies to keep their business afloat under any circumstances.

In the future, everything will change, except customers' eagerness for great experiences. The fast-paced, technology-driven world today is only going to get faster and more disruptive, creating new trends in customer experience. Understanding the direction where customer experience is headed will help companies make the necessary adjustments today to stay relevant and excel in the future.

Here are several future trends companies should pay attention to and prepare for.

Agile Human Automation

Automation can serve customers quickly anywhere, anytime. Humans can offer outside-the-box solutions and provide the emotional interaction and personal touch that many customers crave and often need. The future is about companies having successfully achieved a symbiotic integration between humans and automation. Working holistically, side-by-side, to effectively fulfill customers' needs and demands.

Hyper-personalization

Companies are moving from one-size-fits-all customers to one-size fits-one customer. Personalizing the service to accommodate specific individual needs, preferences, and limitations is already expected by customers. The future is about hyper-personalization. That is, changing the offering according to a customer's life events. Being alongside customers, understanding the situation they are in, limitations they have and offering them the best possible options for that moment. Creating a bonding relationship that customers enjoy with a company they praise.

360-degree Transparency

Transparency has always been a critical component in service because it's a key ingredient in building trust. 360-degree transparency is about making the entire customer journey clear, open, and flawless. It's about letting customers know what will happen every step of the way. Answering their questions, being accountable for service failures, having responsible business practices and providing the necessary information customers need to make proper and accurate decisions.

360-degree transparency requires everyone in the company to make sure every decision or offer made, is communicated and explained to customers in a coherent and truthful way.

Data Protection

As more personal data is gathered by companies, data protection becomes a top priority. Companies have to show customers that data protection is a core issue by displaying unequivocal efforts taken to secure their information. Companies can use technology to make sure legislation like GDPR (General Data Protection Regulation) and other impending privacy legislations and regulations are followed to a tee, avoiding needless data breach as well as regulatory and customer backlash. In 2022, the average cost of data breach globally has reached an all-time high of $4.35 million [1].

Keeping Valuable Customers Enthusiastic

The competition is intense and only getting more contentious. Disruptor companies are appearing in every industry. They come with new, shining offerings that are aimed at catching the eye of other company's most valuable customers. Protecting these VIP customers has to become a major part of every company's future strategy. They have to constantly reinvent their service offering for customers already maxed on the company's perks. They have to develop advanced, unique, and cost-effective ways to keep them happy and enthusiastic about the company.

Service Pairing

Service providers and customers are people. Obviously. People get along with some people and less with others. They collaborate and communicate well with people similar to themselves. In service, a similar situation happens. Some service providers like to interact, talk, and serve certain customers more than others. Those they like, receive great experiences and those they like less receive a lesser experience.

Today, service providers are randomly paired with customers. In the future, new softwares will pair service providers and customers who have similar characteristics. By analyzing the customer's as well as the service provider's history of interactions, profile, and preferences, the software increases the chances of successful pairing, resulting in more positive interactions and more delightful service experiences.

Individual proactivity

Reactive companies wait for customers to make contact and only then deliver the service. The company and its service providers are on an endless treadmill of requests and customers waiting on hold. Proactive companies initiate the contact with customers to control and enhance the relationship.

The future is about companies moving toward individual proactivity. The company analyzes the database to find customers whose proactive actions will benefit them the most. Consequently, getting the best possible results for both sides.

Smart 24/7 Interactions

In today's mobile, on-demand world, the customer can be anywhere in the globe and need help at any time of the day. "Regular" opening hours and "after hours" rarely fit the customer's busy schedule and thus become irrelevant. Having service providers work around the clock and answer questions in the middle of the night is problematic.

With remote working, the company can have people in different time zones and different countries around the world who will be ready to answer questions at a "normal time" wherever they are. The system will route the customers' contact details to the available service provider who are equipped to address the customer's concerns. Smart, timeless, 24/7 service contacts.

Targeted Content

Customers are bombarded with information. The amount of content that customers are exposed to just keeps on growing. As a result, when customers search for specific information, they often feel like they are trying to find a "needle in a haystack" and they are frustrated. Feeling they are wasting precious time in-vain.

In the future, companies will have to provide summed-up content that gives customers the most relevant and important points. Then, offer an option for customers to delve into and read more on any chosen topic. The content should be customized to fit each customer's specific needs and should be presented in various forms for customers to choose from — video to see, text to read, or audio to hear.

A Real Personal Assistant

The rise in the use of voice assistants such as Alexa, Siri, and Contra has been exponential with billions of users. However, these devices are currently used mainly for the most basic options — alarm clock, playing songs, etc. In the future, companies have to think about how they will use these assistants to help and guide customers along their journey with the company. Voice activation frees up customers' hands, eliminating distraction, reducing mistakes, and providing more personal and engaging experiences.

Video Feedback

Feedback has historically been provided through writing or talking. With YouTube, TikTok and Instagram, video is more popular than ever. Especially with young people who are prospective customers.

In the future, companies will ask customers to use video for feedback or problem resolution. Video enables customers to show what they need or the problem at hand, rather than provide a lengthy explanation. This is a more simple and convenient way. When customers use video for feedback, the company can see emotions, facial expressions, and other visual cues — information that helps understand the depth of the customer's grievance. Allowing a better preparation for handling the situation, adjusting behaviors, and choosing the ideal treatment.

Conclusion

Walt Disney said "Times and conditions change so rapidly that we must keep our aim constantly focused on the future." The winds of transformation in customer experience are getting stronger. Transformations that used to happen every five to ten years are now happening every year or two. Future success depends on adapting to the trends presented above and making the necessary transition. That is the key to staying relevant, continuing to drive value for customers, and delivering great experiences for long-term success.

Reference

[1] Hill, M. (2022). What is the Cost of a Data Breach? *CSO*. Available at https://www.csoonline.com/article/3434601/what-is-the-cost-of-a-data-breach.html

Index

www.ingramcontent.com/pod-product-compliance
Lightning Source LLC
Chambersburg PA
CBHW060237220326
41598CB00027B/3961